Origins Of
Secret Societies

Also by Richard Stevko:

Visual-Literary
ABSURDITIES
ABSURDITIES II
THE GHOST TREE – collaboration with Tamara Stevko

Anapoetry - based upon poetry
CONTRASTS
WHERE THOUGHTS COME FROM
BEYOND A PERSIMMON
TURNABOUTS

Mental Archaeology - formerly known as philosophy
SHADES OF MEANING
MENTAL FUNCTIONING
NEUROPHYSIOLOGY
BEFORE PHILOSOPHY

Memorial
TASTE OF THE TATRAS

Origins Of
Secret Societies

Richard Stevko

The Graven Image, Publishing
Hampden, Massachusetts

First Printing: 2017

ISBN 978-1-365-71788-8

Publishing Company
Name: Lulu
Address: 3101 Hillsborough St, Raleigh, NC 2760
Phone: (919) 459-5858

to preview or to order publications:
 http://www.lulu.com/spotlight/rstevko
 http://www.lulu.com/spotlight/stevko

or contact
www.gravenimagepublishing.com

Origins of Secret Societies
CONTENTS

INTRODUCTION

Secret societies and/or their precursors have probably existed since prehistoric times. As written information was unavailable, warranty had to be found in other forms of evidence. The earliest historians accepted legend and word of mouth; still a favored method of communication and teaching. The structure of hypothetical secret societies is presumed from hearsay, verification implied from persistent legends, patched together with reports that have been revealed by the exposers[1], and enlarged by additional inferences that fit random data and have not been disproved. Recently, archaeological and genetic information has been used to substantiate what had been little more than a guess.

In ancient times, much like the present, people who possessed a breadth and depth of information not readily available to the population at large were not only shown respect for their knowledge, but also presumed to hide abstruse information, raising wariness of covert connections. This latent prejudice gave rise to a form of autogenous unease / fear / paranoia that considered the information dangerous, if political, and magical if transcendent. Whether gained stealthily or by extraordinary effort / study, there was, and often is still, a lack of discrimination between the Unknown and Magic. The distinction that separates Religion from those two, and further, from meta-physics, has not yet been satisfactorily drawn.

That prejudice was probably absent in primitive societies and immature thinkers, due to naive

---

[1] who have broken the vow of secrecy required of all initiates.

neurological systems which matured, in a new way[2], during the evolution of sub-tribe: Hominina, genus: Homo. As a matter of fact, as philosophy[3] evolved, cognate forms clearly exist between Western, Hellenic philosophy and Eastern, Vedic philosophy [see NOTES GAINING KNOWLEDGE]. The Greeks made more of an effort to separate the knowledge from the myths; whereas, for the Indians, only the Upanishads, the closing part of the Vedas, were philosophical in the Greek sense. The other parts are, to the Western mind, religious (rituals, ceremonies, benedictions). To the Eastern mind, these are defined, in the ancient Sanskrit, as knowledge.

The earliest recognized wise men were the Magi and the Druids. Every cultural region probably had an analogous esoteric group. The Magi are widely remembered through early written sources (e.g., Bible, Gilgamesh). The Druids are known through comparable sources (King Arthur, Celtic legend). They were revered directly as keepers of esoteric knowledge probably secondary to the depth of their knowledge in Math, Astronomy and detailed Observations of Nature regarding seasons and the cycles of weather occurrences, plant growth patterns, and medicinal properties. Due to their astute observational abilities, they were also familiar with wildlife and human behavioral patterns. This made possible their prophetic abilities. The indistinct line between information and knowledge led many to

---

[2] May not have been entirely new, but the increase in complex circuitry seems to have contributed more than in the past, when increased mutations seemed to demand increased size.

[3] one of the results of brain maturation.

unwarranted use of knowledge; like astrology and alchemy.[4] One notorious practitioner who made illicit use of data was Simon Magus, cited in The New Testament, Acts 8:9-24.

The difference in meaning has shrunk between *esoteric* and *recondite*:
• esoteric - refers to the security of the knowledge
• recondite - refers to the difficulty of the knowledge
Though both are difficult to understand and easily misinterpreted; they both refer to the same knowledge, but to different methods of availability. Esoteric knowledge may be deliberately unavailable until one traverses prerequisite levels; Recondite knowledge is hidden by its intrinsic complexity until one has mastered the fundamental levels.

Secret societies, when discussed today, usually lead to conversations entangled with conspiracy theories, paranoid ideas, or just plain lack of information. That statement is not meant to be critical of legitimate suspicion, or skepticism. The notion of secrecy is antithetical to our cultural character; but that conviction is constantly in balance with our fealty to privacy. Understanding is also confounded in the meanings that have attached to many of the notions used in discussing this topic:
• Secret v. Mystery
• Learn v. Know.

----

[4] astrology and alchemy are not to be taken as false forms; indeed much of modern personality studies and chemistry are based on their early findings; nevertheless it was easier for charlatans to take root in them, much as "quack" physicians did in the early days of commercial electricity.

CONFUSING CONCEPTS *i*
Secret / Mystery

SECRET It is worth the effort to review the concept of secrecy, especially the mental components that seem to require it, and the reasons that engender it; if only to become attuned to how our mental state shapes and is shaped by it.

Secret Societies? What an oxymoron - a figure of speech that includes two seemingly opposed terms, producing an incongruous, allegedly self-contradictory effect. Granted we all have secrets, but we don't band together around them, as central foci, into societies. One meaning shade of *secret* is *hidden*; two kinds of concealed secrets come to mind - private and group.

- PRIVATE SECRET is usually a ploy to avoid unease. To avoid public display of an incomplete mental process, before it is dressed up and ready to go out, is a sign of self-respect and consideration for others.
- GROUP SECRETS (another oxymoron) usually hide covert intentions, and usually are not benevolent. Even gossip is at heart an innocent socialization, though often thought of as being exclusionary and can become toxic . What we know of secretiveness (for our purposes, hidden knowledge) has more dimensions worth exploring.

The Simple Definition [M-W DICTIONARY] of *secret* lists the following senses:
- a fact or piece of information that is kept hidden from other people. (concealed)
- a special or unusual way of doing something to achieve a good result. (reserved)
- something that cannot be explained. (unknown)

In the first sense, the fact or piece of information kept hidden is presumably something already known, as there has to be someone *keeping* it hidden; and it is thus known by the keeper of the secret. If it is a thing, not yet known, why build of a unique category, *secret*, to add to the definition? If that which is hidden is indeed a fact or piece of information, that implies that it is not unknown. Both fact and information are precursors of knowledge, and are categorically similar (see below: Ackoff senses of knowledge) The ambiguity created by this situation may shed light on why the word secret carries an ominous cachet. This should be clarified; and will be addressed in the section *Further views on what it is like to have knowledge*.

In the second sense, *a special or unusual way of doing something to achieve a good result*, covers the establishment of guilds, modern industrial espionage and military secrets. Today:
- a person of scientific bent, would assume that the Unknown is simply that which remains undiscovered and will be known through the scientific method;
- the person of religious bent would assume the Unknown is unknown to Mankind, but not to the Creator, and will be revealed by Divine Intervention. This has traditionally been called a mystery. a philosopher, such as [WITTGENSTEIN§309], who can rises above the physical and metaphysical assumptions is able to shift paradigms, set a new category.

Much of this seems a long way round to flesh out much of what is already common knowledge. It is pursued in such detail to underscore that much of the original meaning of the words is related to the time in which it was found necessary to manifest the linguistic birth of the notion, and all the aggregate meanings cohering to it from the common knowledge out of which it emerged.

The third sense, *something that cannot be explained*, assumes that in the category of *Unknown*, there is a subcategory of *Unknowable*. The modern usage would imply that the secret is hidden information known by at least one person. The mystery is unknowable hidden information. Two analogies of regicide, drawn by [ADELMAN] from Shakespeare, describe the pathway to becoming king. King *Richard III* was known, by his henchmen, to be capable of attaining his goal by murder; whereas in *Macbeth* it was unknowable by anyone, including Lady Macbeth and himself, whether or not he had that capability. In these examples, Richard's intention was a secret; Macbeth's was a mystery.

MYSTERY: Always there have been people who felt it incumbent on them to guard the standards of culture. These groups have been in existence since ancient times. They were people who felt, having attained information, that it could have been dangerous in the wrong hands[5]. Such guardians of information, though they wanted to disseminate their knowledge, often kept core concepts secret, had members graduated into stratified levels of accomplishment (ranging from initiates who were taught exoteric secrets to adepts who gained full esoteric knowledge).

Long before the day that these formal teachers held forth their doctrines, the knowledge upon which they

---

[5] this has not only meant clandestine, but also mis-interpretable on basis of insufficient understanding.

depended had been accumulating in the public consciousness, when myths were not held simply as fanciful products of imagination, but as knowledge of the first order, the best explanations of the unknown available to Mankind. Though we look back and refer derogatorily to myths as news without substance, we seldom reflect on how myths are formed, nor recognize the process in modern myths. Many myths begin with legends. The legend grows into a myth when it serves to unfold part of the world view of a people and embodies the ideals and institutions of a society

- story - an account of incidents or events
- legend - a story which has grown from alleged historical roots into a traditional story
- myth a traditional story that unfolds the world view of a people or explain a practice, belief, or natural phenomenon. a popular belief or tradition that embodies the ideals and institutions of a society or segment of society
- mystery - Something difficult to understand without specialized knowledge. A religious belief based on divine revelation, especially one regarded as beyond human understanding.

Many of these Mysteries had roots in and were transformations of contemporary myths reflecting certain archaic aspects of common Indo-European religion, with parallels in Indi-Iranian religion.[JANDA, M.] [HALL, M.P.] The three most prominent mysteries in the Greco-Roman world were:
the Eleusinian Mysteries (Demeter and Persephone),
the Dionysian Mysteries (Bacchus and Ariadne), and
the Orphic Mysteries (Orpheus and Eurydice).

There are experiences so profound that it actually takes some degree of personality reconstruction to accommodate to them. Whether *life-changing* events are conventional (marriage, parenthood, advanced education), or unique (divorce, grief, combat), it is hard to share the intensity of that event with someone who has not undergone it. Indeed, even sharing it with a veteran of the experience sometimes seems banal; requiring detail sufficient to border on maudlin and analogies that fringe flippancy. Although there is a significant difference between the experienced and the naive, no two adepts have had exactly the same experience; especially since contacting the same external events does not cause the same perception in each.

Nevertheless having had a transformative experience binds people who have shared it, and tends to initiate reluctance, even refusal to divulge happenings which they feel are important enough to have in some way changed them (other potential life and death encounters either by enhancement or diminution of what they consider an important part of their Selves). Researchers, who find verification to a hypothesis, who discover a thing previously unknown, realize the difference in how the information is received by colleagues (with similar backgrounds) and the public, whose understanding is based on inadequate understanding. Creative accomplishments, when shared, always leave the artist with some degree of emptiness.

Before the periodic table and the planet Neptune were demonstrated, they were unknown entities, and as such were secrets [a]; when they were demonstrated they became secrets [b]. They would not possibly be mysteries, unless as secrets [a], they were indemonstrable, and as such, unknowable.

	Entity	confirmation claimed
secrets [a]	unknown	deductive
secrets [b]	demonstrable	objective
mysteries	indemonstrable	subjective

'Dark matter' and 'planet 9' have not yet been demonstrated, but are knowable indirectly by the gravitational influence they exert on their environments. That influence is measurable, constant, and consistent with the laws of physics (therefore being rational - subject to reason). Other observed phenomena (e.g., supernatural), are not subject to laws of nature[6] (and are therefore arational - not subject to reason). A third category, *irrational* - negation of reason should not be confused.

---

[6] The Necessitarians' non-theistic view of Laws of Nature surreptitiously preserves the older prescriptivist view of Laws of Nature, namely, as *dictates* or *edicts* to the natural universe, edicts which – unlike moral laws or legislated ones – no one, and no thing, has the ability to violate. [SCRIVEN]

CONFUSING CONCEPTS ii
Learn / Know

LEARNING is so extensive a process that entire disciplines are devoted to it: education, epistemology, and major parts of psychology, systems management and computer science. This topic has previously been reviewed [STEVKO 2013 MENTAL FUNCTIONING]. It is not the intention here to explore learning, per se, but to clarify the consequences of a common practice, i.e., the interchangeability of verbs and nouns. To convert a verb into a noun is simple and so widely accepted, it intuitively feels right. An action word run becomes a thing (noun, as a state of being) by adding -ing; as do action words fly and swing (flying, swinging). The reverse, noun to verb, is also simple: add -ing to a noun and shoulder becomes shouldering (as in "shouldering the burden"), or more simply using the noun as a verb (as in the military drill command "shoulder arms") and allow the context to shoulder the burden of meaning.

Linguists feel that the original meaning of the verbs, learn (*process of acquiring information*) and know (*ability to recognize*) have been flattened through common use as nouns (gerunds[7], infinitives[8]) to now mean the same thing: body of organized information. But as past participles, they still also mean "currently acquiring information" and "the current state of possessing information." Clarity has clearly not been

---

[7] learning, knowing

[8] to learn, to know

served; indeed, it is further degraded by the addition of *learnage*[9] as a parodic equivalent of Knowledge.

The two words, *learn* and *know*, may be in the same ontological category (verb), but are not in the same category of activity. *Learn* as in *I learn x* has the sense of *acquiring* something; *Know* as in *I know x* has the sense of possessing *something*. Also see [NOTES Grammar]

The word *knowledge* has two senses, in its popular use.
* sense 1 - a body of information (most commonly used; derived from sense 2).
* sense 2 - a capacity for learning (original notion, historically).

The Anglo-Saxons used two distinct words, *witan* and *cnawan*, for these very different meanings. Other languages[10] continue to use two or more words to clarify meaning. [HARPER]

[ELIOT] was one of the earliest to recognize a hierarchy of information
Where is the Life we have lost in living?
Where is the wisdom we have lost in knowledge?
Where is the knowledge we have lost in information?

---

[9] urban dictionary

[10] German *wissen, kennen, erkennen* and in part *können*; French *connaître, savoir*; Latin *novisse, cognoscere*; Old Church Slavonic *znaja, vemi*

DIKW

[ACKOFF] largely popularized the DIKW hierarchy:

Concept	Basic constitution
Opinion	Raw material (indirectly available)
Data	Raw material (directly available)
Fact	Data mediated by sensory system
Information	organized facts (seen in context)
Knowledge	information used in situations
Understanding	evaluated knowledge
Wisdom	evaluated understanding

Raw material, which is not directly available is usually construed as *ding an sich* (see f.n.14)

Structurally it has evolved through many versions; see [Notes DIKW]. Philosophically, it has many problems, mostly ontological, but in information circles is a popular model.

This organizational scheme is stimulated by the existence of historical linguistic categories (which respond flexibly to changing situations); but based on modern pragmatic adaptations. It is demanded by flexible, impermanent language; it needs a rigorous format to aid understanding. It seems that is an advantage particularly well suited to our assessment of learning. At the moment we will assay whether or not it fits our needs, by focusing on the changes that occur in facts when they become knowledge, and try to clarify that new structure (fact/knowledge).

DATA are of two categories, based on derivation - sensory and ideational. If we view derivation of data sequentially rather than coincidentally, all data is first derived from sensory information and processed, sequentially, in the central nervous system as ideas. Ideas are then available as sense data, further processed, coincidentally, as association data in concert with other stored memories, to form beliefs or opinions (unverified facts).

FACTS are the building blocks of learning. A fact is not an object but a representation of the existence of an object (symbol). The meaning of the word, *fact*, lies in the way speakers of the language agree to use it [WITTGENSTEIN§43]. They are real entities, warranted by sensory experience and verified by the agreement of all others' experiences with the same object. Any disagreement must be resolved by affirming the integrity of the declaring senses. Disagreements between intact sensory systems re-categorize the disputed facts as opinions.

Any direct [RUSSELL] unmediated [KANT 1781] experience[11] of the entities, is considered impossible. All challenges of falsifiability needs to doubt the claimant's perception, as it is equally impossible for disputers to have more direct evidence. This caveat becomes especially important in discussing abstract

---

[11] Called *noumenal* by Kant. (e.g. known in itself [*ding an sich*, self-evident] rather than mediated by the senses); considered unknowable by Kant.

facts. So, facts are unorganized observations, and are static (a bound condition).

INFORMATION is accumulated facts in context. A tree, in itself, has no meaning to us. That does not mean it's not important; but, by itself, it is not known to exist. That it can exist without our warrant, makes it unknown to us. It becomes a fact when we sense it, perceive it, certify it. It becomes information when it, and other facts, are seen in a context that differentiates the tree from other objects (organization). In fact there are some thinkers who would say we created the tree, or at least, what we call a tree out of the orderly structure of molecules interacting with the soil, the sun, the environment to photosynthesize energy.

KNOWLEDGE is information used in a situation, and is dynamic (created out of use). We have already noted the use of this word as equivalent to an accumulation of information is misleading in that information and knowledge are different ontological categories; information being static, and knowledge being dynamic; information is something you get, store, use, etc., and knowledge is the use of that information for some purpose. Customarily used to answer the question *How?*

UNDERSTANDING is knowledge that has been evaluated and abstracted. It can be applied to many situations. It is valued against other information that has been warranted, against application in other situations other than the one in which it was formulated. As such is creative. It is also evaluated against the understanding of others. Prosaic examples of this are: handyman / engineer, farmer /

agronomist, accountant / mathematician, introvert / philosopher. Appreciates the question, *Why?*

WISDOM is evaluation of understanding. As such it usually entails understanding over a broader range; and is usually interpreted as a higher consciousness.

====

John [Dewey] proposed a complex alternative hierarchy. He and Arthur Bentley, American philosophers, arguing that "knowledge" was "a vague word", presented a complex alternative to DIKW, including some nineteen "terminological guide-posts". [PLATO Divided Line] earlier proposed an analogy to discriminate notions stimulated by sensory means from more considered information. Ironically, this notion could as well be used to attack his doctrine of *forms,* as to support it.

Other examples of understanding in which knowledge is surmised:
• as Mendeleev did in 1869 with hypothetical elements in the periodic table
• as the influence of gravity was noted leading to the discovery of Neptune in 1846
• as 'dark matter' was presumed by Jan Oort in 1932
• and as 'planet 9' is presumed in 2016.

The wave function of gravity was in this category until 2016. See below in section on Further views on what it is like to have knowledge
Other perspectives in the section: Development of Knowledge - Mysteries.

Part I
Learning Process

THE LEARNING PROCESS

Introduction

Why do we know something rather than nothing?[12] This question is meaningless, as posed. If it is possible to know, at all, it is not possible to know nothing and still pose the question; it reduces to "How do we know anything?" Does the mix of data entering our minds simply mix and match chaotically? The matrix out of which data produces concepts follows in this section and in [NOTES GAINING KNOWLEDGE]. Ideas recorded by principle thinkers varied over the years, and are summarized in [NOTES DUALISM]; and placed in historical context of particular thinkers in [NOTES BIOGRAPHIES].

Why do we know many things rather than everything? This question is meaningless, also, unless we are willing to consider things as facts rather than beliefs. Sorry, theologians and philosophers, this is the world in which we live, and with which we need to deal. Appreciation is extended to artists, who, in their creativity, have embedded glimpses of the unknown for all to share without subscribing to opinions cloaked as facts.

To further complicate the issue, the two questions are actually much different than they seem. The first question involves the virgin landscape of beginnings; the second, of endings (limits). Questions that begin with the word *why* are usually philosophical questions and in this case imply the need for an ontological answer (defining the terms of the proposition, e.g., the

---

[12] No apologies to Leibniz. It's a question too captivating not to be readdressed repeatedly.

meaning of *know*). Most answers beyond that usually reduce into *how* questions and demand a scientific answer (describing the mechanism involved in knowing).

What is called *knowing* is a state of familiarity with the object; and is comprised of the body of facts, information, and skills available to one's consciousness in order to demonstrate that familiarity. The etymology of the word is revealing: O.E. *cnāwan* 'recognize, identify,' from PIE root **gno-* "to know". The development of these roots can almost be pictured as a necessary form to express what furniture is in one's mind in way of cognizing and re-cognizing something familiar. By extension, to know is a state of familiarity, and knowledge is the aspects available to exercise that familiarity. Just having that furniture in one's head does not insure that will happen. A necessary additional step involves the processing of the facts, information and skills - setting that amalgam against information already stored and storing the resultant information for future use.

This fabrication of notions assumes that the interaction depends on an external environment. It also assumes that a protocol is in place for the processing. Such a protocol is called learning. *Learning* and *Knowledge* are often used as synonyms. In this work, we will stipulate [13] definitions:

learning - the process of gaining information and skills (used prominently via the sensory system); and the process of converting that information and

---

[13] assigned meanings to build a clear model without the entanglement of conventional usage; subject, of course, to redefinition after the model has served its purpose.

skills into knowledge (used prominently in perception and in reflection).

knowledge - use of information and skills.

These stipulations are necessary in this context, as the specified words have assumed a use that is confusing. The basis of this difficulty seems to have related roots that have flourished differently in the East and in the West. see NOTES Gaining Knowledge

Hypothesis of the Learning Process

HEURISTIC - These efforts have been based in mythology, religion, philosophy, etc. and have been limited by the drawing mostly from concepts that are annealed already in mature learning systems. To circumvent the influence of prejudice on the process of learning, per se, and on the resultant knowledge, we should like to attempt a view as free of variables as possible by creating a thesis of the learning process in a newly born child. Beyond that, every individual is responsible for integrating the learning into knowledge. This point will be implicit in the theorem we develop.

INTRODUCTION - The question at hand is whether knowledge is innate or is acquired by experience. This question itself may be faulty. The extent to which the environment influences knowledge is evident to anyone raising children; but things that come out of the blue are just as impressive, and seem to support the concept of innate knowledge as well.

As we make our way through each day, we are surrounded with things, and we spend a lot of infancy and early childhood defining them[14]. In the biological sense, we are them - made from the same stuff - and as we individuate, becoming more complex beings than that of which we are constituted, so we differentiate the characteristics of our surrounding matter and see them become distinct.

Learning Process in Action
I.   data
II.   perception
III.   object constancy
IV.   warrancy (justification)
V.   prejudice
VI.   social certification
VII.   acculturation
VIII.   formalization

THE PROCESS IN ACTION - Our nervous systems are well adapted for learning. They first discover and then define[15] the objects in our environment. That process is involuntary in the beginning. The objects' presence in our environment is not initially voluntary on their part, either. They exist, we exist. Their presence becomes known to us through our senses, a gift that has been granted us by the process of evolution as a condition of survival. Those beings that developed sensation continued to survive due to their increased ability to interact with the environment. To those who object to this statement on the basis that our sensory systems are fallible, the replies are: 1) you are right,

_____

[14] Actually, they may define us, especially in the beginning. (after the views of Kant and Chomsky)

[15] The separation, classification or categorization necessary in defining is at the basis of Taxonomy. See Notes Classification

2) they are good enough to get us to the moon and back, 3) whatever other systems are involved in learning, they work integrally with the sensory system.

I.DATA The learning process seems primitive at first; the apparent simplicity is deceptive. On first confronting the world, the consciousness of a newborn receives signals from its new environment, which it has never seen[16] and cannot recognize the objects in it (having never cognized them before). Though it may have an intact sensory system, the data is totally unknown and essentially constitutes chaos. The discovery simply requires the objects emanating signals that are received by the organs of sensation. The emanation of signals is not a Sci-fi phenomenon, but the result of the atmosphere being awash in particles and waves that bounce off the objects and register upon our sensory receptors. Those receptors absorb the waves and particles which are converted into electrical signals. Done.

Well, not quite! The new information is not simply tallied and stored by a homunculus. The biological underpinnings of consciousness, the brain, has been working, not only since it was formed; but as part of its formation. Its complexity[17] of meaning and usage is increased by what the organism does by adjuncts[18] and by perception. But initially, in the environment, the

---

[16] *See* is used here as a synecdoche for all the senses.

[17] perception. Also note that the infant is not tabula rasa, but has perceived much in the uterus. Raises the questions of stages of development and stages of accomplishment. When does one begin perception?

[18] telescopes, microscopes

infant is aware of objects by sensory means [19]: seeing, hearing, tasting, smelling or touching. Awareness is the beginning of learning. An object simply is or is not there. Questions as to whether it exists when it is not there, do not occur; nor do its other manifestations or morphs.

II.PERCEPTION For that notion to occur the existent thing must have been processed in the brain, comparing it to other similar or identical beings: a process that is part of perception. The electrical impulses into which waves/particles are transformed is the language of the brain (could be coined as neuron-speak, brain-speak or mind-speak).

Whether or not the impulses translated in the mind as the object is a true representation of the object is open to question. We know that our sense organs record only a portion of the spectrum to which it is sensitive; bees for example see flowers differently than we do. Dogs hearing spectrum is different than ours. Bats "see" sonar metaphorically. If we speak metaphorically, musicians claim to "see" the world in sound.

Mathematicians assert the world is numbers. Artists feel colors. Synesthesia may be an extreme form of this phenomenon, but we all share some degree of appreciation for the cross fertilization of senses. But metaphoric comparisons deflect us from our purpose. What we are calling metaphors, if they are metaphor, may simply be the best way we have of

---

[19] That is one clue to the level of development in learning. Compare learning by rational means. Another level entirely. see Notes

understanding what they represent; and as such may be as close to truth as we ever get.

III.OBJECT CONSTANCY When two objects are registered in the brain as *the same*, the learning organism is presented with options:
• accept them as the same object at different times
• accept them as two similar objects
• accept them as different objects.[20]
In either case the representation of the object is stored, pending further evaluation, which results in differentiating (categorizing) them. These options are not apparent in the beginning; they result from the involuntary[21] learning process revealing many aspects of the object that are reliable differentiation points. Some of the most important points, aside from identifying physical characteristics (such as mobility, number of feet, and other primitive traits), are some subtle attributes (such as are the objects present at the same time or in the same place). These last points are essential concepts that give the infant the notion of object constancy - an essential cognitive step in ego development.

---

[20] a fourth option, ignore-ance, occurs in certain circumstances. It has been discussed by [STEVKO Mental Functioning]

[21] This is not meant to be an ethical statement, but a note of ability. Free choice or Voluntary activity usually implies motor activity (though not always); free choice requires choosing an unbound direction - assuming choices - requiring information. The choice itself is a more advanced learning process.

IV.WARRANCY[22] After one has accumulated enough learning points (data) then one can chose to accept the objects as the same or different. In this process the learner has learned to collect data, process it, and make decisions about it. The process has creative aspects. The category of that object has been created. Subsequent encounters with similar objects will either expand that class (into dogs of various sizes, colors or breeds), or create a new class (other quadrupeds). Essentially the learning process has forced definition of the category; epistemology has created the need for ontology, in this case.

Does this process work in reverse? Can the nature of an object's being (ontology) create the manner in which it learns (epistemology)? Of course it can. We have just demonstrated that. The learning process we have just described (an actual description of an actual organism, actually learning) is possible only because of the nature of its being. Indeed, the nature of its being and the manner of learning are connected. Neither would exist without the other.

V.PREJUDICE Were we to define the world in atomic terms, it is alleged to be mostly space, but that is not strictly true. The space is maintained by electron fields, which have repellant strength and prevent the object from collapsing in on itself. The whole field of chemistry is based on perceiving the world as composed of atoms...leading to the periodic table,

---

[22] A warrant is a sign of justification. Warrancy is coined here to indicate the state of possessing qualities that support being warranted.

fields of force, valence, etc. The space we can measure is not empty.

The force fields that inhabit them seem to create action at a distance, an illusion, as we are not tuned to perceive the electromagnetic forces occupying that space.

In subatomic terms, the structural components are things like quarks, bosons and other quantum particles; the bodies upon which the forces discussed above act. In the ordinary world, in which we live, the everyday which is not augmented by science - a world that is changing into the science enhanced world (which is *natural*, which is the everyday world of people who have trained into scientists[23]) - in this science un-augmented world (or what is left of it); in the world inhabited by children and animals, the project of learning goes on. The innocent beings perceive objects as we see them in picture books. These are the objects that [PLATO, *Republic*] called *shadows* (of ideal *forms*), that [ARISTOTLE, *Metaphysics*] called matter plus form.

As the infant learns about these objects, if he is told they shadow something else that has reality in an ideal world, that child is prejudiced to think like Plato; if he thinks the substance is real, but composed of intangible characteristics, then that child is prejudiced to think like Aristotle. See more in NOTES GAINING KNOWLEDGE and NOTES PREJUDICE IN LEARNING

VI.SOCIAL CERTIFICATION Just as one grows into knowledge, just by being an intimate in a family; so

---

[23] just as people have trained into mathematicians, musicians, artists, etc.

does one grasp that other families have information that is not in the data base of one's own circle.This information may not be deliberately hidden, but may simply be a function of what it is like to be a different family. It may be something as obvious as having a sibling of a different age, or none at all.

With continued growth one comes into contact with ever wider circles, expanding the amount of what is unknown, allowing for a greater number of facts accumulated, as well as a substantial increase in information which is the relationship between the facts. Not only the information gained through informal experience, but that from the entire educational system, is based on that premise as is the apprenticeship system.

Ironically, while passing through the system and gaining increased knowledge, if your expectation had been to gain satisfaction, the reality is that that satisfaction comes with a price - that body of facts carries with it new questions; as wisdom [OED, MW, ACKOFF] unfolds novel insight. As we attain increasingly complex acquisitions: facts, knowledge, insight, and wisdom, each step not only builds our mental library, but reveals the pastures of wildflowers yet to be gleaned.

VII.ACCULTURATION. No one ever knows everything. This was noted, differently, in the Introduction to The Learning Process. What is knowable[24] is too voluminous. As mankind developed

---

[24] The facts are too voluminous, concepts even more so, and as we expand into the realm of the abstract, knowledge is less certifiable and epistemology becomes more of a preoccupation

the ability to reflect on the enormity of what remains unknown, that which became knowable had, in the past, been secret or mysterious. The discovery of knowledge often accompanied contact with knowledgable individuals, who were perceived as revealers of secrets, and, by extension, keepers of the mysteries.

The search for knowledgable individuals in hunter-gatherer societies was for relatively concrete things - to learn to hunt, you accompanied hunters, and were taught the skills for successful hunting, tracking, etc. To learn abstract concepts is a little more difficult. The people maturing in the time must have had at least three categories of influence on them. One would have been, as in any learning, direct experience. The second would have been the influence of authorities (which in the case of family could not have been very distinguishable from the first). The third level of influence would have been other members of the society[25], that may have included, or been subordinate to a formal designated officer (such as a priest or shaman). Though it has always gone without saying, that there is information even beyond the designated officers, the public began to lose sight of the difference between the hidden and the unknowable.[26]

In the course of things, several feelings arose:

---

[25] this is referred to as a level rather than category since the progress of the categories is, as in all learning, sequential in time and in increasing degree, surely a larger circle of acquaintances less responsible for primary care-taking

[26] Both the hidden and the unknowable are reifications of the unknown. see [Notes reification]

- the sense of being excluded
- the assumption that mysteries were not unknowable, but occult
- the expectation that there were those "in the know"
- the giving to the knowers an authoritative position
- the predication that access to the mysteries was available

The search for knowledge proposed so far has focused on individuals living in a family or small group, but by the time the third level of influence was accomplished by a designated individual, it seems plausible that the group has socialized into a larger community with cultural standards, and those may have included individuals designated with other specific skills, e.g., healer, astronomer, alchemist. Many of those individuals would have acquired skills and insights beyond the reach of ordinary members.

Many of those skills and insights were gained, not by aptitude alone, but by granting to capable candidates preferential support of the leaders, thus allowing devotion of time to further study in areas not available to the general populace. As a result, those who held knowledge not generally available were held in higher esteem by others as holders of special knowledge.

VIII.FORMALIZATION.The emphasis so far has been on the learner. The earliest teachers had been family; later, tribal members; finally, formal teachers. Aside from the formal teachers so far mentioned (shamans, priests) there were more formalized teaching methods. In Ancient times, hired tutors (such as members of the Sophists, Stoics in Greece) or itinerate teachers (such as Socrates, Christ, Buddha). Both before and after the itinerate teachers, there were groups that tutored and individuals or groups that helped establish and taught in academies. Throughout Medieval Times education gradually became more formalized and universal - by training of clerics in monasteries, who then taught publicly; the insistence of Protestant individuals like Luther and Calvin to make scriptures available in the vernacular; and by the establishment of universities.

As the formal teachers became more esteemed, they would find ways of devoting time to the advancement of their discipline. This happened both in consultation with colleagues, in challenges by students (initiates), or within one's own research and reflection. In any event, the most abstract and esoteric ideas were shared and challenged with a bicameral [JAYNES, J.] method by thinking about others thoughts or thinking about one's own thoughts.

When these thoughts centered about concrete objects, the group was called a guild,
When these thoughts centered about abstract objects, the group was called a college,
When these thoughts centered about mysteries, the group was called a religion[27].
However the actual development of those organizations occurred in the opposite order; presumably the need to address more abstract topics is driven by greater anxiety.

---

[27] Originally, the most esoteric groups were religions; but two things changed that: the difference between religion and philosophy has still to be established in the conventional wisdom; the difference between clandestine and esoteric has still to be established in the conventional wisdom

Further views on what it is like to have knowledge

The novice learner has a subjective view, from inside the head, that there is a world of objects out there, to be collected, processed into data and used. The same learner has also had the experience of sensing familiar objects (i.e., things seen before, ostensibly already filed into memory, or remembered, by our present understanding), and conversely sensing unfamiliar things (things inconsistent with data storage; i.e., not remembered) and, by the way the neurological system is wired[28], has felt discomfort, leading to curiosity, or avoidance. The result is that the learner learns by experience that there are things already learned and things yet unlearned. The seed is planted.

One other possibility exists - facts sensed, but not contextualized as information, leave an imbalance in the homeostasis of neurological processing. That processing needs to culminate in knowledge; failure to do so stimulates other emotional and volitional categories of processing, a bridge that cannot be burned without consequence. An imbalance that suggests the existence of a third category, the Unlearnable.

If this notion prickles the reader's sensibility, it should. The idea that there remains something unlearnable does not fit into the thesis so far; but the above allusion to direct and unmediated experience is as thorny a topic if the references to Russell and Kant are pursued.

---

[28] connected to the emotional systems.

Likewise, our hypothetical learner, if unable to successfully convert unknown fact to knowledge, may fail to pursue the sequence of events that complete that adaptation. They are at risk of repeatedly being discomfited every time it comes up. A willful adaptation would likely be used; an avoidance; an inauthentic determinism maintained at some psychic cost.

Some has come in and is mine, the rest needs to be learned and will be mine. There is a different attitude, called objective. It is held by someone who has already learned a lot; realizes there is still a lot to learn; and furthermore realizes that some of what is unlearned is also unlearnable.

That seems paradoxical. How can someone who has not learned a particular thing, be familiar enough with it to judge its learnability? There are things, admittedly that no one knows. We think that's right. No one has questioned everyone in the world to see what they don't know, and would not be able to list those things unless the questioner knew of their existence. If we ever find the person that knows something everyone else considers unknowable, then that one thing has been falsified as an unknowable. This did happen recently when the wave function of gravity was demonstrated On February 11, 2016, the LIGO[29] Scientific Collaboration and Virgo[30] Collaboration teams announced that they had directly detected gravitational waves from a pair of merging black holes

[29] Laser Interferometer Gravitational-Wave Observatory.

[30] a giant interferometer, located near Pisa in Italy, designed to detect the gravitational waves that Albert Einstein's general theory of relativity predicts. Named after Virgo constellation.

using the Advanced LIGO detectors. [CASTELVECCHI] [ABBOTT] [NSF].

Yet, we are compelled to ask: How were they able to pinpoint that particular unknown? Someone must have known, in some way, that there was an unknown to be known. They blame it on Einstein. What was his inspiration? Whence came his knowledge. In the billabong of answers, two prominent areas emerge: Divine inspiration and deductive reasoning.

- to the Divine inspiration group, the challenge is - did not *The Divine* cause humankind to develop reasoning powers?
- to the reasoning group, the challenge is - did not *the laws of nature* cause humankind to discover the universal power of those laws?
- to both groups, the challenge is - what's the difference?

The difference seems to be the primacy that each group places upon the origin of their knowledge in preference to their method of adding to that knowledge. Furthermore, the difference is no less than the difference between theology and science. Both disciplines look at the unknown and are inspired to create the best explanation for what they see. That explanation must make sense to their peers to become widely acceptable. It also must be alterable if demonstrated to be unfounded.

The mechanism of knowledge's origin and its expansion must be the same or else one of the mechanisms is suspect. Knowledge of entities knowable through the senses (tangible objects) is increased by data collected through the senses; knowledge of ideas (abstract notions) knowable through thought is increased through further thought. Sense based knowledge, at the entry point into consciousness must become ideational, formed as ideas, rely on what we call thought. The question arises - does abstract knowledge, that knowable through thought, originate in the mind, or is it sensory based?

This controversial topic, innate knowledge, was not soluble by the ancient philosophers and has remained intractable through the ages. In modern times, notions of self-evident knowledge has included ideas that include hard wiring (language), complex instincts (nest building), and VMAT2 (humans who carry this gene are hypothesized to be predisposed to religious, spiritual and non-rational faith-based decision making that disregards logic and scientific reason). [SURRATT]

PREFACE REDUX

After Mankind became civilized enough to live in groups larger than the clan, after the concept *barely adequate* became the notion *parsimonious* and after some members became proficient enough in some skills to expect it is somewhere between sensible and mandatory to barter part of the harvest for that person's artisanal output or skills; then it became acceptable for the craftsperson to specialize in lieu of toiling soil.

The specialists gained the conceptual space to develop their craft, and occasionally teach apprentices. It was the teaching, surely, that forced contemplation of not only the how-to of the craft, but to organize the integrated body of knowledge that lay behind it. This body of knowledge integrated years if learning, years of practice, and years of innovation to make up for what was not known and to integrate new innovations into a rigorous practice.

Perhaps it was the knowledge, contemplation, experience and research that built an unaware facade that impressed the clansmen as being beyond the ken, as being above average, as being even super natural. They began to suspect the craftsmen and apprentices as harboring secrets (which the artisans did, in a way). As the community grew enough to support multiple competitive craftsmen, each protected themselves from what is known today as industrial espionage. A wayward apprentice in the shop of a rival was capable of revealing the best flint sources for making spear heads and methods to stop that could ranging from guilds to individual methods which in themselves were secret.

Eventually, the guilds (organizations to protect the interests of members) became collegial societies as the craft-groups were comprised of members with knowledge that was beyond the usual person's understanding. This event was not so much an act of authority as of necessity for colleagues to be able to discuss matters of concern without the distraction of having to be spend time accommodating those who have not done the groundwork of understanding.

Though the community needed and appreciated the guild members and collegians, there was always a modicum of resentment, not only for what they perceived as the withholding of secrets, but also for what was perceived as the roots of deference, seen into the future as not much different than the compliance and obeisance demanded by the aristocracy.

The word *mystery* had a theological and a secular meaning [HARPER]:
- theological - hidden (except to God), unclear (to man)
- secular - occupation

The secular sense gave the name Mystery Plays to religious tableaux staged by members of craft guilds. The two senses of the same word gave rise to theatrical punning in the Tudor period. It is entirely likely that the association of the meanings also contributed to the association of *mystery* with *occupation* and the ominous meaning of secret societies. Today, the words *secret* and *mystery* are synonyms, but, as has been explored in a prior manuscript [STEVKO 2013 SHADES OF MEANING], synonyms seldom mean exactly the same thing. In this case, the words are similar in the sense of *hidden*, but are dissimilar in the sense that *secret* is a more general term, and that which is kept secret is a *mystery*.

Other origins can be traced to ancient Greece when Plato, in his dialogues, *Meno* and *Phaedo* refers to membership in Eleusian societies. This and other ancient secret societies are discussed below. The concept is also in the New Testament [KJV]:
- John 12:16 "These things understood not his disciples at the first: but when Jesus was glorified, then remembered they that these things were written of him, and *that* they had done these things unto him."
- Luke 18:34 "And they understood none of these things: and this saying was hid from them, neither knew they the things which were spoken."

- Matthew 17:13 "Then the disciples understood that he spake unto them of John the Baptist."
- John 16:12 "I have yet many things to say unto you, but ye cannot bear them now."

Plato and Christ, at least in their teaching techniques, apparently had much in common. Plato used the Socratic method and Christ spoke in parables. At heart, they both seemed to have the purpose of guiding people to understanding the mystery of reality, without fencing in and flattening out the concepts. Both fencing and flattening limit meaning, in that fencing excludes aspects that are essential to the expressed meaning, and flattening restricts the fullness of meaning in each concept. For example, a definition can be restricted by disallowing some synonyms on the basis of quantity; or it can be deprived of fullness by disallowing some synonyms on the basis of quality. a synonym doesn't mean exactly the same thing. a synonym has meanings unconnected with the index word.

Plato and Christ are commonly interpreted today as not having spoken plainly, and couched their interpretations in dualistic terms; though both, as shown above have claimed to not have been clearly understood; both claiming that additional teaching was necessary to have the full mystery revealed. Socrates, on the other hand, avoided writing for a similar reason. He tells a story about the discoverer of the use of letters being informed by the king, to whom he presented it as a gift for the people.

> "...this discovery of yours [use of letters]
> will create forgetfulness in the learners'
> souls, because they will not use their

memories; they will trust to the external written characters and not remember of themselves. The specific which you have discovered is an aid not to memory, but to reminiscence, and you give your disciples not truth, but only the semblance of truth; they will be hearers of many things and will have learned nothing; they will appear to be omniscient and will generally know nothing; they will be tiresome company, having the show of wisdom without the reality.

...writing is unfortunately like painting; for the creations of the painter have the attitude of life, and yet if you ask them a question they preserve a solemn silence. And the same may be said of speeches. You would imagine that they had intelligence, but if you want to know anything and put a question to one of them the speakers always gives one unvarying answer. And when they have been once written down they are tumbled about anywhere among those who may or may not understand them, and know not to whom they should reply, to whom not: and if they are maltreated or abused they have no parent to protect them; and they cannot protect or defend themselves." [PLATO, Phaedrus]

As far as secret societies are concerned, I have no direct knowledge. Having been in positions which have required effort to reach, I have been accused, by those who did not make that effort, of having secret connections; and been asked to provide others with the same imagined influence. Conversely, there have been many of good heart who have lauded success without envy, have congratulated without seeking credit, even when they have contributed. They have been modestly encouraging, usually in proportion to the accomplishment.

There are many ways in which an individual may seem to have connections that seem secret to others. Indeed, any knowledge that is not shared widely will seem clandestine to the uninformed. When asked to share the experience with people who have not participated in the same endeavor, it is impossible to bestow it satisfactorily; even those who took part in a similar enterprise seem to lack sufficient resonance. What is it about some kinds of knowledge based on experience that makes it difficult to understand?

The answer may be simpler than the question makes it seem. In a prosaic sense the answer is contained, and not hidden, in the precept that the way to get to Carnegie Hall is practice, practice, practice. Those three simple directions (or single uber-direction), if followed faithfully, assume the acquisition of knowledge and, if done thoughtfully, the attainment of understanding. This statement is not a new age, kumbaya raising of consciousness, but an old fashioned, hard work method whose only secret is the necessity of commitment for success.

It is not only the motor skills that require the repeated experience to achieve the automaticity of flawless performance (so called muscle memory), but the repeated use of critical rationality hones thinking skills as well. The Chinese Brush Painting master, Ning Yeh, recognizes this connection, beginning his classes with a Tai Chi type admonition. Sit straight in the chair, both feet squarely on the floor, straight back, straight arms, straight mind. Yet, this is not just occult oriental wisdom; your grammar school teachers had similar counsel, which unfortunately most took as a rebuke. That's not having a straight mind.

The idea, *Mens sana in corpore sano* [JUVENAL], is usually translated as "a sound mind in a sound body", and is mostly quoted as an admonition for physical exercise, but has often been used to promote intellectual endeavors to athletes. To quote it hierarchically is to miss the point that though mind and body can be trained independently, the secret is in the interaction; if it's a secret that is still sought, the answer lies in the experience of rigorous mental and physical exercise.

Emergence of Mystery Religions

The role of experience in learning has been debated [Notes Gaining Knowledge]; and came to a head most conspicuously between Plato and Aristotle. To Plato, the ultimate reality was knowable only through reason and reflection, and it resided in ideas or eternal forms. Aristotle claimed that ultimate reality is knowable through experience, residing in physical objects, and his writings were often based on first-hand observation.

In trying to bridge this division between them, others became apparent. At Plato's death, Aristotle (who would seem, to us, to be the natural replacement to head the Academy) was by-passed in favor of Plato's nephew, Speusippus. His lineage was surely justified on the basis of blood relations, but a greater difference separated them. [PLATO], and apparently Socrates, [31] were initiates in the society of Eleusinian Mysteries, Aristotle was not. Aristotle wrote that 'those seeking initiation do not so much learn anything, as experience certain emotions, and are thrown into a special state of mind.' [SYNESIUS]

Descriptions of the Eleusian initiation ceremony vary. They range from the reverential [PLUTARCH] to emotive (Aristeides' experience of sensations from horror to joy) [CASAVIS]. The following account by Synesius indicates that Aristotle took the same position:

> "But their procedure is like Bacchic frenzy - like the leap of a man mad, or possessed - the attainment of a goal without running the race, a passing beyond reason without the previous exercise of reasoning. For the sacred matter (contemplation) is not like attention belonging to knowledge, or an outlet of mind, nor is it like one thing in one place and another in another. On the contrary - to compare small and greater - it is like Aristotle's view that men being initiated have not a lesson to learn, but an experience to undergo and

---

[31] Whether or not Socrates was an initiate is implied both ways. see [NOTES BIOGRAPHY]

a condition into which they must be brought, while they are becoming fit (for revelation)." [SYNESIUS]

Characteristics of Mystery Religions [MORFORD]

Christianity shares many characteristics with other mystery religions of antiquity, which are called mystery religions because of their concern with the fundamental mysteries of human existence: life and death, questions about god, the soul, and the afterlife. Also, these mysteries involved secrets revealed only to members of the religious group, the initiates.

> "...these Mysteries possessed many fundamental likenesses; (1) All held that the initiate shared in symbolic (sacramental) fashion the experiences of the god. (2) All had secret rites for the initiated. (3) All offered mystical cleansing from sin. (4) All promised a happy future life for the faithful." [ENSLIN]

Part II
Ancient Mysteries

Ancient Mysteries

Most of the ancient mysteries evolved from myths. Myths being a poetic expression (metaphors, in this case) of widely held beliefs. A belief is built up from repeated coincidences (numerology, astrology); as such is the most broadly accepted explanation of natural phenomena, and expanded into rituals that celebrated, recognized and encouraged the mythic characters. The implications of those rituals were complex, leading to informed, knowledgable teachers (hierophantes) who could explain and interpret them. A hierarchy of learners (initiates, mystae) and advanced learners (seers, epoptes) evolved as a formal society. [BRITANNICA] It was this hierarchy that laid the groundwork for the transferral of mysteries to learners in secret societies. "The Lesser Mysteries are a preparation of the neophyte for initiation in the Greater Mysteries through various degrees of purification and discipline combined with training in intellectual and spiritual perception." [KNOCHE]

Nature, as stable as it seems, is riddled with phenomena that yield surprises. Mankind is irked by the unexpected, and seeks understanding. Still, as always, the best explanation had to do, until a better came along. This sentiment has been noted both in the artistic and the scientific world: "Good reasons must of force give place to better." [SHAKESPEARE]; "Those among us who are unwilling to expose their ideas to the hazard of refutation do not take part in the scientific game." [Popper]. In the pre-scientific era, the interpretation was usually in the form of a myth; scientifically, it's a deduction. Both groups were, and are, doing the best they can with that which they work.

Incongruous natural phenomena and the resultant myths make up these Mysteries, divided, for ease of presentation, into Epochs, Geography and Archetypes:

EPOCHS - not well defined time spaces, but cohesive durations during which the listed cults flourished
• Primitive
• Ancient
• Classical

GEOGRAPHY - The form that the rituals took was determined by local influences as much as mythological creation. These do overlap the ancient and classical epochs. examples
• Zurvanism
• Canaanite religion
• Druids
• Norse mythology

ARCHETYPES - characteristically reifications, and sometimes deifications, of concepts that appeared in mysteries. Some of the earlier mysteries also fit archetypes, but less well [KERÉNYI]
• Great Mother (Dea Syria)
• Lesser Gods (Cabiri)
• Mytheme

Primitive Epoch Mysteries

Indo-European religion
Proto-Indo-Iranian religion
Vedic / Puranic (Hindu)

Indo-European religion	
Origin - reconstructed from cultural remnants of the Indo-European peoples.	

Characters	Principle:
Dragon / Serpent	Common in most Indo-European mythologies battle -> hero / god slaying a serpent / dragon [WATKINS]
Sun	metaphor for •sunrise / sunset •freedom / imprisonment related to •dragon slaying •cyclical events.
eclipse	metaphor for destruction / rebirth related to being eaten by demons
Brothers	two progenitors of mankind [ANTHONY 2010]: *Manu*- ("Man") and *Yemo*- ("Twin")
Bulls	mythic bovine creatures common
Other myths	see P.I.E. religion

Proto-Indo-Iranian religion
Origin - an archaic offshoot of Indo-European religion; preceded earliest Hindu and Zoroastrian scriptures.

Characters	Sanskrit	Avestan	Principle:
*rta	rta	asha	the universal force
*sauma	Soma	Haoma	sacred plant / drink
*mitra	Mitra	Mithra	gods of social order
*bhaga	Bhaga	Baga	lord, patron

Persian cult of Mithra Vedic god of oaths personified by sun Mitra-Helios

Narrative: reified spirits
Explanation: a spirit "worthy of reverence"
   iconography includes:
• being born from a rock
• slaughtering a bull
• sharing a banquet with the god Sol
Evolution: syncretized into distinct Roman Mithraic
Mystery society. Probably competitive with christianity

Vedic / Puranic (Hindu)			
origin - India			
Characters:	Principle:	Hindu	Vedic
Prajapati	divine triad	deities group	creator
Brahma	creator		
Vishnu	preserver		
Shiva	destroyer		

Ancient Epoch Mysteries

Osirian Cults
The cult of the Apis bull
The Cult of Isis
The Cult of Serapis

Osirian	
origin - Egypt	
characters:	principle:
Osiris	ruler of all the earth
Isis	Queen of Light
Seth (Typhon)	Spirit of Darkness Brother of Osiris
Horus	Son of Osiris and Isis

Narrative: Osiris, Isis, and Typhon (Seth) were born out of the midst of chaos [APULEIUS] [READE]. Their mother was Nut, whose body arched from horizon to horizon (sky), and their father was Geb, whose body is the Earth, lying beneath her. Osiris, ruler of all the earth, was murdered and mutilated by his jealous brother, Typhon, who usurped the throne. Isis retrieved the body, reassembled its parts and , with the resurrected Osiris,conceived a child, Horus, who triumphed over Typhon and re-established order in the kingdom. [ASSMANN][WILLIS]

Explanation:

The two Deities, Isis and Osiris were seen as the parents of all the Gods and Goddesses of the Heathens, or were indeed those Gods themselves worshipped under different names. Elements of the story serve as archetypes for other mythologies; Sira is said to have mutilated Brahma, just as Typhon did Osiris; and Venus is said to have lamented her slain Adonis, just as Isis wept for her husband-god.

As yet the sun and moon alone were worshipped under these two names. And as we have seen, besides these twin beneficial spirits, men who had begun to recognize sin in their hearts had created an Evil One who struggled with the power of light, and fought with them for the souls of men.

Evolution: Cognate Names

Origin	Sun	Moon
Egypt	Osiris	Isis
Persia	Mithra	Anahita
India	Brahma	Isi
Phoenicia	Baal or Adonis	Aphrodite or Venus
Greek	Apollo	many
Norse	Odin	Frigg
Briton	Hu*	Ceridwen**
Celtic		Islene or Aisling***
Lapland / China	Baiwe /	Puzza

Ishtar, Demeter, Ceres, and Isis are all one [PLUTARCH], and represent living matter, or matter vivified by spirit, which is a doctrine of the Mystae

Now worshipped throughout the whole world, though under different names. [READE]

- Isis also received the names of Islene, Ceres, Rhea, Venus, Vesta, Cybele, Niobe, Melissa--Nehalennia in the North; with the Indians; among the Chinese; and among the ancient Britons.
- *Hu - spirit, that hidden behind the sense-world.
- **Ceridwen (pronounced [kɛrˈɪdwɛn] *Cer-id-wen*) was an enchantress in Welsh medieval legend. She was the mother of a hideous son, Morfran, and a beautiful daughter, Creirwy. Her husband was Tegid Foel, and they lived near Bala Lake (*Llyn Tegid*) in north Wales. Medieval Welsh poetry refers to her as possessing the cauldron of poetic inspiration (Awen) and the Tale of Taliesin recounts her swallowing her servant Gwion Bach who is then reborn through her as the poet Taliesin. Ceridwen is regarded by many modern Pagans as the Celtic goddess of rebirth, transformation, and inspiration.
- *** Aisling - dream, vision, inspiration

The Cult of Isis	
origin - Egypt	
Characters:	Principle:
same as Osirian	same as Osirian

Narrative:
This cultic development is, as above, dependent on the story of Osiris, Isis, etc.; but focuses more on the posthumous separation and reconstitution of Osiris' body parts. The Osirian myth had its beginnings in the Delta region. As the cult of Isis spread rapidly up the Nile towards Nubia, Osiris gained prominence, became identified with the funeral god, and assumed the title, King over the Dead. Isis' role in caring for Osiris' remains gained her prominence in the rituals.

Explanation:
Egyptian belief, from primitive times, was that the body had to be preserved in order for the soul to survive death. The rituals of burial and passage into the afterlife had been restricted to the pharaohs, only, based on politics and laws related to ownership and inheritance (regarding power and property). During the sixth dynasty, rights were extended to the aristocracy. After the dynasty fell, this practice gradually extended to the common people as well. The Isis cult appealed to Commoners and provided access to eternal life for them, too.

Evolution:

To the people of Ancient Egypt, Osiris was their means to eternal life, and this was achieved by copying the exact forms and rituals of his embalming. The entire mummification process put the deceased through the same trauma as Osiris himself had to endure. The body was taken away from the home to "the place of purification."

"Osiris' identification with eternal life, with life from death, gave rise to his mystery cult which would travel beyond the boundaries of Egypt as the Cult of Isis. Although no one knows what rituals were involved in the mystery cult of Isis, they may have developed from Osiris' earlier mysteries celebrated at Abydos beginning in the Twelfth Dynasty (1991-1802 BCE). These were very popular festivals which drew people from all over Egypt to participate in the ritual. Bunson notes that "the mysteries recounted the life, death, mummification, resurrection, and ascension of Osiris" (198). Dramas were staged with the major roles given to prominent members of the community and the local priests who enacted the story of the Osiris myth.

Harmony and order had been established by the son of Osiris, Horus, and the king was Horus' living representative who provided for the needs of the people. Osiris was credited with establishing both the kingship and the natural order and law of life and so, through one's participation in one's community and observance of rituals, one was following Osiris' guidelines. The people, as well as royalty, expected the protection of Osiris in life and his impartial judgment after death. Osiris was the all-merciful, the forgiving, and the just judge of the dead who oversaw one's life on earth and in the afterlife." [MARK, J. J.]

The cult of the Apis bull	
origin - Egypt	

character	principle:
Ptha	created the world (conceived by Thought; then realized by Word)
Apis	embodiment of Ptah intermediary between humans and all-powerful god*

*originally Ptah, later Osiris, then Atum

Narrative:

Apis worship began early in Egyptian history. [MANETHO]

Explanation:

After death Ptah became Osorapis, i.e. the Osiris Apis, the embodiment of Ptah (Apis) was assimilated to Osiris, the king of the underworld.; a bull might ritually represent a king who became a deity after death. He was entitled "the renewal of the life" of the Memphite god Ptah

Evolution:

There were three great bull cults of ancient Egypt, Apis being the most popular. The worship of the Apis bull was continued by the Greeks and after them by the Romans, and lasted until almost 400 A.D. Osorapis was identified with the Hellenistic Serapis, and may well be identical with him. Greek writers make the Apis an incarnation of Osiris, ignoring the connection with Ptah. Ptolemy I (Greek pharaoh) created Serapis, the official anthropomorphic god of Egypt and Greece a common religious base to unify the two peoples and ease tension in the country [THE NEW ENCYCLOPAEDIA BRITANNICA]

Classical Epoch Mysteries

Mithraic
Chthonic
Eleusinian
Orphic
Dionysian

Mithraic	
origin: Persia	

character:	principle:
Ahura-Mazda (Ormuzd)	Spirit of Good
Arimana	Spirit of Evil
Mithra	communicator (cognate for Hermes)

Narrative - Ahura-Mazda brought forth a number of hierarchies of good and beautiful spirits Angels Archangels. (one of which was Mithra)
Arimana good and beautiful, but rebelled in jealousy; became Spirit of Evil, in consequence. Not even aware of Ormuzd, before light created. Mithra is the Zoroastrian angelic Divinity of Covenant and Oath

Explanation:

"The doctrinal premises are

    (1) good will eventually prevail over evil

    (2) creation was initially perfectly good, but was subsequently corrupted by evil

    (3) the world will ultimately be restored to the perfection it had at the time of creation

    (4) the 'salvation for the individual depended on the sum of [that person's] thoughts, words and deeds.

There could be no intervention, whether compassionate or capricious by any divine being to alter this.'

Thus, each human bears the responsibility for the fate of his own soul, and simultaneously shares in the responsibility for the fate of the world." [Boyce]

Evolution:

"While the Mithraic mysteries succeeded those of Zoroaster, they followed those of Dionysios, through which the core of Hellenic mystery teaching found its way into the Western Mystery Tradition. Two streams of consciousness are discernible within the Classical mysteries, which might be called Dionysian and Apollonian. The Apollonian mysteries related to reason, to the heavens and to order; this is in contradistinction to the chaotic, ecstatic mysteries of Dionysios." [Rice]

Mystery Chthonic	
origin - Sumerian(S)/Akkadian(A)	
character	**principle**
Dumuzi(S)/ Tammuz(A)	god of food and vegetation; a pastoral deity consort of Inanna/ parallel consort of Ishtar
Inanna(S)/ Ishtar(A)	(S) version, goddess of love, infamous for ill-treatment of her lovers/ (A) version, goddess of love, fertility and warfare.
Ereshkigal	Sister of Inanna/Ishtar ruler of underworld
Ea	Father of Tammuz Babylonian version of Noah

Inanna also has a very complicated relationship with her lover, Dumuzi, in "Inanna's Descent to the Underworld". She is associated with rain and storms and with the planet Venus, the morning and evening star. as was the Greco-Roman goddess Aphrodite or Venus.

Dumuzi/Tammuz - equivalent versions
Beginning with the summer solstice came a time of mourning in the Ancient Near East, as in the Aegean: the Babylonians marked the decline in daylight hours and the onset of killing summer heat and drought with

a six-day "funeral" for the god. Recent discoveries reconfirm him as an annual life-death-rebirth deity: tablets discovered in 1963 show that Dumuzi was in fact consigned to the Underworld himself, in order to secure Inanna's release, though the recovered final line reveals that he is to revive for six months of each year (*see below*). Inanna had gone to visit sister.

The concept of dying-and-rising god was first proposed in comparative mythology by [FRAZER].
He associated the motif with fertility rites surrounding the yearly cycle of vegetation and cited the examples of Osiris, Tammuz, Adonis and Attis, Dionysus and Jesus Christ. [METTINGER]. [THOMPSON] categorizes many of these motifs see [MOTIFS]

Eleusinian	
origin Greece	

character:	principle:
Demeter	the earth goddess
Persephone	her daughter
Hades (Pluto)	god of the dead

Events:
Hades, in love with Persephone, snatched her away to his underground (chthonic) abode. Demeter petitioned the gods, who ruled that Persephone must stay with Hades 6 months of every year but would be allowed to return to Demeter for 6 months every year. Demeter, in her joy, allowed flourishing when Persephone returned

Explanation:
explained how the seasons rotated and the principles responsible (Persephone's interaction with Hades and Demeter: liaison between forces of life and death)

Orphic	
origin: Thracian	

character:	principle:
Orpheus	bard, son of Apollo and Calliope, the muse
Eurydice	Orpheus wife

Narrative:
The omens, at his marriage, were bad, and the new bride was bitten on the ankle by a snake and died. The grieving Orpheus was so inconsolable that he dared to descend to the Underworld, where he made his appeal to the king and queen themselves, Hades (Pluto) and Persephone (Proserpina), in a song sung to the accompaniment of his lyre. In the name of Love, Orpheus asked that his Eurydice be returned to him in life; if not, he would prefer to remain there in death with his beloved. His words, his music, and his art held the shades spellbound, and the king and queen were moved to grant his request, but on one condition: Orpheus was not to turn back to look at Eurydice until he had left the Underworld. As they approached the border of the world above, Orpheus, anxious and yearning, turned and looked back, through love. At his gaze, Eurydice slipped away from her husband's embrace with a faint farewell, to die a second time.

Explanation:
It is rewarding to compare the poetic emphasis of the two (Ovid and Vergil) and analyze the reasons for variations in incident, drama, and purpose; both, in different ways, immortalize the theme of tragic love and devotion. Through music and poetry and with extraordinary art, he delivered a persuasive religious message, the foundation of a mystery religion called Orphism. This message is linked both to Apollo and to Dionysus, gods often antithetical in nature. Orpheus is torn to pieces by fanatical Bacchic maenads; this mirrors the fate of Pentheus and suggests that his death was prompted not only by his sexual rejection of women but also because of the nature of his religious teaching.

Evolution:
With its myth of creation, the Orphic bible was linked in some of its details to the Hesiodic account but differed radically in its spiritual content. The first principle is Time (Chronos) and Eros, or Love, is the first born of the deities, called PHANES [fa'neez] and hatched from an egg. Fundamental for dogma was the myth of Dionysus (see MLS, Chapter 13), in which the infant god was torn to pieces and devoured by the wicked Titans; from the ashes of the Titans (smitten by Zeus' thunderbolt), humans were created; hence the immortality of the soul, sin and virtue, reward and punishment.

Dionysian	
origin uncertain. (Thracian, Greek or earlier)	

character	principle
Dionysius/ Bacchus	son of Zeus and Semele son of Zeus and Persephone god of wine, emotion
Ariadne	consort
multiple	consort
Hermes	took infant Dionysius to hide him from Hera
Wine	discovered by Dionysius; impetus for emotions.

Narrative:
- Gk. version - born again from thigh of Zeus, after Semele burnt to cinder on seeing Zeus in full glory (Hera'a trick)
- Cretan version - born again from thigh of Zeus, after Titans, induced by jealous Hera, to rip apart Dionysius were destroyed by Zeus who saved only the heart

Explanation:
his death and rebirth were events of mystical reverence

Narrative:

Ariadne version 1 - After Ariadne had helped Theseus navigate the labyrinth to kill the Minotaur, she was abandoned by Theseus and saved by Dionysius.

Ariadne version 2 - Dionysus descended into Hades and brought Ariadne and his mother Semele back. They then joined the gods in Olympus.

Explanation: The vine of Dionysus became a symbol of renewed life and Christian resurrection and redemption.

Narrative:

Hermes version 1 - gave to Ino, to raise as girl, thus deceiving Hera.

Hermes version 2 - taken to the rain-nymphs of Nysa

Hermes version 3 - given to Rhea, or to Persephone to raise in the Underworld

Explanation:

In Dionysian mysteries, discloses why his origin is unknown and why he was a late entry to the pantheon.

Narrative:

Mature Dionysus discovered viniculture; but Hera struck him with madness, and drove him forth a wanderer through various parts of the earth.

Explanation:

He brings happiness and salvation to those who accept him peacefully, and madness and death to those who do not. By extension, uncontrolled use of alcohol led to fertility, theatre and religious ecstasy. His festivals were the driving force behind the development of Greek theatre.

Evolution:

[BURKERT] categorizes him as a dying-and-rising god, a motif occurring so often in folk tales that it has a motif number in [THOMPSON]. The concept was first proposed by [FRAZER] in his comparative mythology where associated the motif with fertility rites surrounding the yearly cycle of vegetation, and cited the examples of Osiris, Tammuz, Adonis and Attis, Dionysus and Jesus Christ.

> "Dionysus, with the emotional din and clash of his music and the unrestrained freedom and passion of his worship, is often presented in direct contrast to Apollo, god of the lyre's disciplined melody, reason, and self-control. These two antithetical forces of the irrational (Dionysian) and rational (Apollonian) are dominant archetypal motifs inherent in human nature, and they have attained a particular importance and influence because of Friedrich [NIETZSCHE]'s study of drama entitled *The Birth of Tragedy*." [MORFORD

Geographical Mysteries

Zurvanism
Caananites
Druids
Norse Mythology

Zurvanism	
Origin: Persia (Zoroaster)	

Character:	Principle:
Zurvan	Boundless Time and Boundless Space
Ahura Mazda	"Wise Lord." - the universal and pervasive source and fountain of all life.
Spenta Mainyuhe	the Holy or Bountiful Spirit
Angra Mainyu	the Destructive or Opposing Spirit

Narrative - Zoroaster (Zarathustra) was a Persian prophet. author, and founder of Zoroastrianism, from which Zurvanism sprung. Zurvan is regarded as being without gender (neuter), without passion, and one for whom there is no distinction between good or evil. Indeed, many think Zurvan may have been a primordial hypothetical construct, from which Ahura Mazda sprung. It would no be too much of a stretch to find cognative ideas between Zurvan / Ahura Mazda and Yahweh / Jesus Christ.

Explanation - Zurvan is the parent of the two opposites representing the spirit of good and the spirit of evil.

> "The words "good" and "evil" are used to describe these two principles, but they are not the best words of description; the key is given in the most ancient Gâthâs. Good and evil may be said to only come into existence when man in his evolution develops the power of knowledge and of choice; the original [Page 26] duality is not of good and evil, but is of spirit and matter, of reality and non-reality, of light and darkness, of construction and destruction, the two poles, between which the universe is woven and without which no universe can be." [BESANT]

Zurvan is also the god of destiny, light and darkness. and strengthened dualism in personal belief systems.

Evolution - Magi, principle format for all esoteric knowledge. Influenced Canaanite religion, as did Egyptian thought; both being influential neighbors.

Canaanite religion

Canaanite religion - Early Canaanite religions, like other Ancient Near East religions, were polytheistic.

> "At the center of Canaanite religion was royal concern for religious and political legitimacy and the imposition of a divinely ordained legal structure, as well as peasant emphasis on fertility of the crops, flocks, and humans." [NOLL] [MOSCATI]

Geographically located between Egypt and Mesopotamia, Canaanite religion was influenced by those religions. Conversely, Phoenician sailors probably carried by Canaanite religious ideas west influencing, e.g., the tripartite division between the Olympians Zeus, Poseidon and Hades, in Greek mythology, reflecting the division between Baal, Yam and Mot, seen in the East.

The words used for God varies in the Hebrew Bible. The form of his name, itself, varied. According to [WELLHAUSEN], the forms, Elohim and Yahweh were used depending on whether the source was Israel (north) or Judah (south)

[MAIMONIDES] said: "I must premise that every Hebrew [now] knows that the term Elohim is a homonym, and denotes God, angels, judges, and the rulers of countries, ..."

Origin of the Druid

ALTHOUGH the term Druid is local, their religion was of deep root, and a distant origin. It was of equal antiquity with those of the Persian Magi, the Chaldees of Assyria, and the Brachmans of Hindostan. It resembled them so closely in its sublime precepts, in its consoling promises, as to leave no doubt that these nations, living so widely apart, were all of the same stock and the same religion-that of Noah, and the children of men before the flood. [READE]

Very little is known about the ancient druids. They left no written accounts of themselves, and the only evidence are a few descriptions left by Greek, Roman, and various scattered authors and artists, as well as stories created by later medieval Irish writers. [HUTTON]
> "Their chief deities were reducible to two--a male
> and a female, the great father and mother--Hu

and Ceridwen, distinguished by the same characteristics as belong to Osiris and Isis, Bacchus and Ceres, or any other supreme god and goddess representing the two principles of all Being." [HECKETHORNE]

[LEIBNIZ] seems to have paraphrased the principles quoted:

"Our reasonings are based on two great principles, that of contradiction… [and] that of sufficient reason." (G II 612/AG 217).

Twentieth Century Druids trace themselves through Masonic literature [Reade] and commercial publications [CARR-GOMM], which, if legitimate, would, by definition, not contain any mystical information, but should have some historical value. There are purported to be three main levels of instruction:

1. Ovate (subordinate instructor) - expected to already know medicine & astronomy and poetry & music to some degree
2. Bard (teacher of wisdom) - memorize 20,000 verses of druidic poetry; takes years to reach this degree
3. Druid (superior instructor) - sees to religious needs of assigned people, level seldom attained. There was, reportedly, a supreme position of ArchDruid.

Odin	
Norse	
Odin	the Allfather
Hel	goddess of the underworld
Geri and Freki (ravenous wolves)	not mere animals but mythical beings: as Woden's followers they bodied forth his might, and so did wolf-warriors.
Ravens Huginn (thought) & Muninn(memory)	Travel the world to bring information to Odin
Yggdrasil	the world tree functions as the integrator of life force and contra as gallows Three roots and each one reaches to a different mysterious world. 1.Asgard, the ancient kingdom of the powerful Norse gods. 2.Jötunheimr, the home of the fearful giants 3.Nilfheim, a place shrouded in primordial darkness, cold, mist, and ice.

Ragnarök Afterward, the world will resurface anew and fertile, the surviving and returning gods will meet, and the world will be repopulated by two human survivors.	a series of future events, including •a great battle,foretold to ultimately result in the death of a number of major figures (including the gods Odin, Thor, Týr, Freyr, Heimdallr, and Loki) •the occurrence of various natural disasters •subsequent submersion of the world in water
Ratatoskr	a squirrel who runs up and down the world tree to carry messages between the Veðrfölnir
Veðrfölnir	Eagle perched atop Yggdrasil
Nidhogg	a dragon who dwells beneath and gnaws at a root of the world tree
Jormungand	the Midgard Serpent

The myths of the Norse Gods spread everywhere the German language predominated, including England.

The mythology of the gods [FAULKES] is easily as extensive as the Greek or Roman myths. This section will deal only with Odin, alone. Though an extensive literature of many deities will not be touched; it will give a succinct view of the themes contributing to esoteric knowledge.

To begin, Odin presides over the welfare of the world; seen in these myths as maintenance of the life force - symbolized by care of the tree of life (Yggdrasil) against adversarial forces that seek to harm it. He needs to buttress the society, and himself, against the prophesied future end of the world as it's known; and he needs, as part of that effort, to tend to his own development: intellectual and spiritual.

The life force that he protects, the tree of life, hosts several residents. At the crown is an unnamed eagle on whom is perched a hawk (Veðrfölnir). Reporting to this sharp eyed pinnacle are two Ravens (thought and memory), who scour the world for useful information, that, in turn, is stolen by a spy squirrel (Ratatoskr) who runs up and down the tree, stealing information and sharing it with a serpent, gnawing on one of the roots of the tree. That root reaches to a mysterious

world deep, dark, misty primordial Niflheim The other root, not as deep underground, reach to Asgard, the kingdom of the Norse gods. The final root is of intermediate depth and reaches Jötunheimr, the home of the fearful giants.

In the tree were also four stags who nibbled at the highest shoots; so there was biological incursion from above and below.

The positive influence his animal companions exerted include a symbiosis observed in the natural world among ravens, wolves, and humans on the hunt

The personal development in which Odin invested was remarkably high. He paid one eye to be able to drink from Memir's well of wisdom. He hung from the tree for nine nights, pierced with his own spear to gain knowledge of the runes. These examples of willingness to pay a high price for wisdom is described more clearly in the Tarot card explanation. See[Notes Hanged Man]

Archetypes

Great Mother
(Dea Syria & other maternal variations)
Lesser gods (Cabiri & other fabulous races)
Mytheme

Great Mother (Dea Syria)	
origin -Syria	
character	principle
Atargatis	chief goddess
Hadad	consort of Atargatis

Narrative:
The Syrian goddess, Atargatis, had her own mythology and an independent cult and became fused with similar dieties to such an extent as to be indistinguishable (Syncretism).

Explanation:
She would have been powerful enough to be seen as the Queen of Gods and the goddess of generation and fertility. In one aspect she typifies the protection of water in producing life; in another, the universal of other-earth; in a third (influenced, no doubt, by Chaldean astrology), the power of Destiny.

Evolution:
The Syrian Atargatis was such a deity, being virtually indiscernible from Ashtart (phoenician), Ishtar (Egyptian), Hera (Gk.) and other deities who were She would have been identified with Aphrodite, by virtue of her role in the emotional aspect of fertility; with Amphitrite, having also originated as a sea deity; and by virtue of her role in the generative aspect of fertility, a great nature-goddess, analogous to Cybele and Rhea.

Great Mother and her lover origin-Asiatic	
character	principle
Cybele	mother goddess
Attis	son - consort

Narrative:

Cybele, a bisexual deity was castrated. From her severed male organ an almond tree grew. She became pregnant from the blossom of the tree placed to her bosom.

Attis was born and grew to a beautiful youth.

Cybele fell passionately in love with him. But he loved another.

Cybele, because of her jealousy, drove him mad.

In his madness Attis castrated[32] himself,

repentant Cybele obtained Zeus' promise that the body of Attis would never decay[33].

Religious ceremonies in honor of Attis celebrated resurrection and new life through the castration and death of the subordinate male in the grip of the eternal, dominant female. The priests were eunuchs called Galli, and rites of initiation included baptism by the blood of a slain bull, the *taurobolium*.

---

[32] see Motif, below

[33] in the sense of remaining resurrectable.

character	principle v. 1	principle v. 2	principle v. 3
Great mother more muted			
origin - Greece, Rome			
Aphrodite, Gk.	Goddess of love	Goddess of love	Goddess of love
Anchises, Trojan	mortal consort of Aphrodite		
Aeneas great hero of the Romans	son of Aphrodite and Anchises;		
Adonis		mortal youth, consort of Aphrodite	
Persephone, Gk. Proserpina, L.			Queen of Underworld

Version 1
- NARRATIVE: Aphrodite (posing as a mortal) seduced Anchises.
- EXPLANATION: Discovering that he had slept with a goddess, feared that he would be enfeebled.

- EVOLUTION: Here is yet again the eternal theme of the Great Mother and the emasculation of her lover, only in a more muted form.

Version 2

- NARRATIVE: Aphrodite fell desperately in love with Adonis and warned him of the dangers of the hunt, but to no avail. While he was hunting a wild boar, it buried its deep tusk into his groin and Adonis died in the arms of a grief-stricken Aphrodite.
- EXPLANATION: The goddess ordained that from his blood a flower, the anemone, should arise.
- EVOLUTION: Here is allegorized the important recurrent theme of the Great Mother and her lover, who dies as vegetation dies and comes back to life again.

Version 3

- NARRATIVE: This motif of death and resurrection becomes even clearer in the following variation. When Adonis was an infant, Aphrodite put him in a chest for Persephone, the queen of the Underworld, to keep. But Persephone looked upon the child's beauty and refused to give him back.
- EXPLANATION: It was agreed that Adonis would spend one part of the year below with Persephone and one part in the upper world with Aphrodite.
- EVOLUTION: Celebrations honoring the dead and risen Adonis share similarities with Easter celebrations for the dead and risen Christ.

To this point we have noted narratives that explain incongruous events. The concept proposed as the explanation is reified as a myth; that, as such, provides a framework for understanding complex events; mysteries that require extended explanations. In the process, reification consists of a stipulation that the hypothetical narrative be regarded as concretely, for the sake of understanding. Likewise, deification stipulates the characters in the narrative are deities or some kind of sacred personage. A large culture can build up an entire pantheon of deities, semi-deities, heroes, and ancillary supernatural characters, good and evil. The reification process has not been improved; it served to create myths and still serves to form hypotheses.

The mysteries may have cohered as mystery religions or secret societies. As time went on, the narratives adapted (as explanations need to, if they are to maintain verity) to changes in various ways. In their earlier form, the abstract concepts of concern were reified into a form with which they could be dealt as though they were concrete, and often even deified. This concretization of concepts made it easy to develop myths with the same theme around a different set of characters. This is easily seen in the Chthonic myths, where Persephone and Eurydice were pursued into Hell (as a metaphor for the summer solstice); and where Dionysius helped Ariadne when she was abandoned by Theseus - resulting in prolific grape harvests. Likewise, a single deity or hero can appear in several myths, demonstrating various aspects of their character. Myths can grow unrestrained in small villages, or accrete many aspects in a large urban setting. Likewise myths can, beside accreting variations, also become syncretic with other myths. Not only can the concept expand as a function of the characters, but the characters can become a reification of the concept, leading to cults dedicated to the idea of groups of deistic entities, e.g., Cabiri.

Mystery - Lesser gods	
origin *- Lemnos, Samo-Thrace	

character	principle
Cabiri	mystic divinities obscure, contradictory [ATSMA]
(Syncretic)	promoters of fertility, protectors of seafarers, blended rites of purification, initiation.

*earlier elements: Hittite, Thracian, Proto-Etruscan (Phrygian)

Narrative:

[AESCHYLUS] - mentioned Cabiri first in a 5th cent B.C drama. Summarized extant fragments:

> "Originally pre-Hellenic chthonian divinities...their cult gradually accommodated itself to the religion of the peoples with which it came into contact ; until, in the historical period, the Cabiri appear as daimones who foster vegetative life and protect seafaring folk, and whose Mysteries in course of time spread over the greater part of the Greek world." [WEIR SMYTH]

It apparently was Aeschylus who first introduced drunken people to the sight of the spectators of 'tragedy'; the Cabiri, coming into contact with the Argonauts in Lemnos, promised them plenty of Lemnian wine.

Cabiric mysteries seem not to have be derived from any singular mythic narrative; but from those of particular peoples in particular places and times. The Cabiric myths began by specifying singular characters in a unique time, but became a collective noun referring to a group, the Cabiri, rather than one Caberus. The functions of that group seem to have evolved into a level of understanding a higher order of mystery than those to which initiates are allowed privy. Generally, commentators grouped the myths.

[Christie] categorized the myths into three groups by the way the name *Cabiri* was used:
- the gods in whose honor the Mysteries were instituted,
- the institutors of the Mysteries,
- the principle hierophants who officiated in them.

[Warburton] exemplified them according to the sense in which each was demonstrated:
1. [HERODOTUS] says, that the Cabeiri were worshipped at Memphis as the sons of Hephaestus, and that they resembled the Phoenician dwarf-gods.
2. [PAUSANIAS] mentions Prometheus and his son Aetnaus to whom Ceres entrusted the Cabiric Mysteries.
3. [STRABO] speaks of the Cabiri as ministers of the sacred Mysteries, in saying the doings of the Samothracian Corybantes are kept secret or are mystic.

In the Samothrace Temple Complex, known as the Sanctuary of the Great Gods, the identity and nature of the deities venerated at the sanctuary was, and remains, largely enigmatic. Apparently, it was taboo to pronounce their names. Literary sources from antiquity refer to them under the collective name of *Cabeiri;* a title or state of being rather than the actual name.

Explanation:
"Much of this is mystical, but it all goes to prove what we began by saying, namely, that the Mysteries were all one, and varied only in the language." [YARKER] After exhaustive, and frustrating research, the narrative of the Cabiri myth remains elusive, despite the many examples listed above, supporting either multiple incongruous stories related to the time and place of telling, or outright denial of any information being available. [Hesiod] clarifies the place of Cabiri in Greek cosmogony. See Notes Cosmogony for a brief review.

Evolution: Though the Cabiri always seem to have been lesser gods, revered for the state of being their personification represented, their archetypical function seemed to have remained stable. In the same way, Syncretism seems to have diffused many aspects of myths; not only changing the names, but connecting mythemes, thereby expanding meanings of the narrative to varying degrees, depending on the explanatory needs it had to fulfill.

Comparative Mythology

GLOSSARY:

Narrative = Story
    ↡
    ↡<-alleged historical roots
    ↡

Legend
    ↡
    ↡<-grown
    ↡

Traditional Story
    ↡
    ↡<-explains world view
    ↡

Myth
    ↡
    ↡<-embodied ideals; difficult to understand
          without specialized knowledge
    ↡

Mystery

ELEMENTS WITHIN OR ACROSS NARATIVES

- archetype (n.) - the original pattern or mode
  - (original)
- cognate (adj.) - allied or similar in nature or quality.
  - (copy)
- theme (n.) - a unifying or dominant idea, motif, etc., as in a work of art.
- motif (n.) - a recurring subject, theme, idea.
- mytheme - unchanging essence, smallest basic unit of a myth; "kernel".

SYNCRETISM - In the course of time, the narratives changed as they were absorbed by other nationalities, new languages, other priorities. All the complications of translation gave rise to new names for the old rites. The Assyrian Dionisu became cognate to the Greek Dionysos, the Latin Bacchus, and the Egyptian Osiris. Other aspects that were bent included comparable ideas, cognate names, generic doctrines.

Syncretism flourished in Rome. Different religions harmonized their gods and myths into some sort of unity. [Morford]. Examples:
• Mysteries that share the same motif:
    • Eleusinian
    • Dionysian
    • Orphic

• Characters that have same function:
    • Demeter/Persephone
    • Bacchus/Ariadne
    • Orpheus/Eurydice

• Egyptian deity Isis [APULEIUS] identity absorbed by similar goddesses:Cybele, Athena, Aphrodite, Artemis, Demeter, Persephone, and Hera

• Activities[34] seen in a culture as related became the domain of one Goddess; and reappeared as a cluster for a cognate Goddess in another culture:
    • Ishtar - Mesopotamian
    • Inanna - Akkadian Sumerian counterpart
    • Astarte - Semitic Aramean cognate
    • Astghik - Armenian cognate

---

[34] fertility, love, war, sex, and power

The characters may be adapted for local reasons:

- Tammuz - consort of Ishtar in chthonic myth. He is named for the month he died in inclement weather; then transported to the underworld. Reversal of roles is not the only syncresis:
    - Gallu demons - a group of minor divinities
    - Ereshkigal, ruler of the underworld, is Ishtar's nemesis and her cognate sister
    - The trials of Ishtar, to regain Tammuz' soul and restore fertility to the earth, are unique in chthonic literature and serve as an exploration of sibling rivalry in ways that would not otherwise be acceptable to the culture.
- Saboz(ios) common name in Hungarian myths probably transformed in Pergamon (Gk. city on Aeolian Sea) by transliteration of Greek alphabet.

Zagreus - Phrygian cults of Rhea / Dionysius
Sicily - "second" Dionysius
One of many[35] syncretizations of Dionysius

---

[35] beyond the scope of this work.

Some categories of Motifs [THOMPSON]
A192   Death or departure of the gods
A192.1.   Death of the gods
A192.1.1.   Old god slain by young god
A192.1.2.   God killed and eaten
A192.2.   Departure of gods
A192.2.1.   Deity departs for heaven (skies)
A192.2.1.1.   Deity departs for moon
A192.2.2.   Divinity departs in boat over sea.
A192.2.3.   Divinity departs to submarine home
A192.2.4.   Divinity departs in column of flame
A192.3.   Expected return of deity
A192.4.   Divinity becomes mortal
A193   Dying-and-rising (resurrected) god
A525.2.   Culture hero (god) slays his grandfather
A560.   Culture hero's (demi-god's) departure
F259.1.   Mortality of fairies

This selection is offered, not as an exhaustive list of motifs, but a sampling of the kinds of recurring ideas used in mysteries and mythology; and are still used in modern culture (literature, religion, moral precepts).

Common Motifs in Mythology

Dying, or departing god/gods	a god* or an entire pantheon** dies or is killed or destroyed
	*Balder (Norse)
	*Quetzalcoatl (Aztec)
	**Ragnarök (Norse)
Castration	"Castration is one of the most universal fears among men. It represents a loss of manhood, of power, and of status. When something is universally (or near universally) feared, it is sure to make an appearance in the various mythologies of the world. All mythologies are stories that connect us to the deeper core of our psyches. Everything we fear, everything we love, and everything we desire is a part of us, and is therefore reflected in the stories we tell." [Schryer]
The world tree (cosmic tree)	connecting the heavens, which it supports, to the terrestrial world, and, through its roots, the underworld.
The tree of knowledge	connecting to heaven and the underworld
the tree of life	connecting all forms of creation

The story element, be it large as an archetype or as overarching as a theme; be it narrow as a metaphor or mytheme often embedded a mystery that required additional explanation:

Element	Mystery
Descent to the underworld (many religions)	Indicates at once the superior characteristics of the hero as well as his impotence to change rules of nature. Represents quest of desired object, tangible or abstract Results in permanent change
The concept of a tree of life (widespread idea in many mythologies)	*sacred tree* represents life growth death and rejuvenation in its annual cycles and broadly in its overall life cycle. Religious and philosophical traditions extend to interaction with environment and life sustaining forces. The expression *Tree of Life* was used as a metaphor [DARWIN] for the phylogenetic tree of common descent in the evolutionary sense.
The hanged man Origin - Tarot card.	The hanged man is not executed but suspended from mundane existence and given position which is both elevated and capable of new perspective. [See Notes Hanged Man]

Element	Mystery
martyrdom of these gods	higher spiritual birth of the twice-born
Saotus or savior [PAUSANIAS]	designated Liberator, and ΥΗΣ.
cabiri (sons of Hephaestus)	mythic genealogy [BURKERT]
a brother slain by his brethren (religious mysticism of all peoples)	the allegory of the self murdered by the non-self
Lesser Mystery [CLEMENT]	*philosophical death*
Greater Mystery	*philosophical resurrection*
twin gods or daimones presided (Samothrake)	over the orgiastic dances of the mysteries performed in honor of the pastoral/chthonic goddesses.

Mysteries were often known by theme (e.g., chthonic), name of principal character (Orpheus), place of conferment (e.g., Samothrace), particular degree of the writer (Hierophant may introduced Bacchus, Lord of the Cross and the pine-cone, while Epoptae may modify same story to Iacchus, Lord of the planet.

Trinities and triads abound throughout myth and religious traditions, such as:

- The triple goddess: maiden, mother, crone.
  - (Kore, Demeter, Hecate in Greek mythology.)
- Two deific principles, and created forms
  - (Egypt - Osiris, Isis, and Horus)
  - (Christian - Joseph, Mary and Jesus)
    - Horus and Jesus named Saotus or saviour to the Mystery-god, and he was designated Liberator, and ΥΗΣ [PAUSANIAS]
- The Christian mystery: Father, Son and Holy Ghost.
- The Vedic trinity: Brahma, Vishnu and Shiva.
- The Vedic creation process: unfolding, maintaining, and concluding (e.g.,birth, life and death.)

Indeed, the triadic formula was embedded so deeply and found to be useful for so many things that it fit naturally into myth and religion. In primordial times, and in some modern cultures, the number 3 is represented by three lines, before the representation of one object by one line is changed to an other symbol (Chinese counting progresses from one to three horizontal lines before changing; Latin progresses from one to three vertical lines before changing).

Chinese 一 二 三 四

Latin   I II III IV

Similarly, many primitive cultures also seem to mentally draw a line between the concepts of the first three numbers and the rest of them, as though things that can be counted fit the category of 1, 2, 3, or more. The idea of *how many* is covered by the categories 1, 2, or 3 for all practical purposes. They knew there were groups larger than 3, but that information had no utility that could not be filled by the designation, *more*. It serves the same purpose as *infinity* does in mathematically literate societies. It is a marker to indicate that beyond which available skills with numbers do not go.

Three, in myths, does not indicate the end of ability, but indicates totality, wholeness, or completion of a concept. It became representative of Divinity, in that sense. In the meantime, the mathematicians were doing unimaginable things with numbers greater than three, or so it seemed. Those who understood advanced mathematics seemed to be wizards to those who still had no use for counting beyond three. Though this advanced math seemed like "occult" knowledge, it was probably at the level of the average high school student today.

Many, like the Greek Pythagoreans, Babylonian and Egyptian architects, Hindu and Chinese numerologists devised ever more sophisticated ways to manipulate numbers and practical applications for those efforts. The myth-makers were sometimes indistinguishable from the numerologist, accountant, mathematician, priest and philosopher. All were, after all trying to explain the Inscrutable. They techniques they employed - ranging from astronomy to astrology; from alchemy to chemistry; from insight to prophecy mostly relied on careful observation of connections, coincidences and causality - found ever more applications for various number concepts to describe previously indecipherable ways to measure, and understand, quantity, structure, space, and change, and, yes,divinity:

perfect number - a positive number that is equal to the sum of all positive integers that are submultiples of it, as 6, which is equal to the sum of 1, 2, and 3. Early occult numerologists considered three as the first perfect number on the basis of being the product of all natural[36] numbers preceding it. This is not a widely accepted mathematical definition.

Three (3) is the first sacred number, the first perfect number. Three represents the Pagan Trinity [WESTCOTT]." It is represented geometrically in the triangle, and spiritually as the Third Eye Of Hinduism.

Four (4) is the first solid number, being the product of three natural numbers. Spatial in scheme or order in manifestation.
As such it is interpreted as static as opposed to the circular and the dynamic. In numerology it has the aura of wholeness, totality, completion and solid. It thus is foundational. Contrariwise, it is the 4th dimension, which is time; and can be illusional.

Seven (7) is a sacred number. [VAN BUREN] calls 7 "one of the most sacred of all the numbers...the Invisible Centre, the Spirit of everything". Since multiplication of seven creates an even more powerful sacred number, we should not be surprised that 3x7, or 21, is considered powerful .

Many of these associations are not verifiable, but, in the context of myth, are accepted as best explanations at the time. Falsification has kept many numerological coincidences from entering empirical

---

[36] positive integers, whole numbers

acceptance; but long term usage, associated with sacerdotal assumptions keeps them in the range of folk wisdom. For example, given the choice of hotel room with the number 7 or the number 13, even the most skeptical person would unthinkingly choose the "lucky" number.

The Concept of Quaternity

The Timaeus, of [PLATO], was the first to propound a triadic formula for the God-image in philosophical terms, starts off with the ominous question: "One, two, three but . , . where is the fourth?" This question is, as we know, taken up again in the Cabiri scene in Faust:

> "Three we brought with us,
> The fourth would not come.
> He was the right one
> Who thought for them all." [GOETHE]

When the fourth was the one 'who thought for them all' we rather suspect that the fourth was Goethe's own thinking function. The Cabiri are, in fact, the mysterious creative powers, the gnomes who work under the earth, i.e., below the threshold of consciousness, in order to supply us with lucky ideas. As imps and hobgoblins, however, they also play all sorts of nasty tricks, keeping back names and dates that were "on the tip of the tongue," making us say the wrong thing, etc. They give an eye to everything that has not already been anticipated by the conscious mind and the functions at its disposal. [JUNG 1975]

According to Carl Jung, Tom Thumb is a personification (contrast with reification) of the creative force. [JUNG 1912] says:

> "We know that Tom Thumbs, dactyls, and Cabiri... are personifications of creative forces... Thus the creative dwarfs toil away in secret; the phallus also working in darkness, begets a living being" (CW5, para. 180)

Mithras was born out of a rock, which, breaking open, permitted him to emerge. This occurred in the darkness of a subterranean chamber. The Church of the Nativity at Bethlehem confirms the theory that Jesus was born in a grotto, or cave. According to Dupuis, Mithras was put to death by crucifixion and rose again on the third day.

These mysteries were considered too complicated to explain directly, and were thought to require even more than extended discussion, needing a sustained[37] influx of information with annotation of an encouraging type and a physiological boost to catalyze it. This last often provided by fasting, special diet, a sustained physical effort, and sometimes a psychedelic reinforcement.

---

[37] sometimes even to the extent or remaining in a certain level (degree), for a prolonged period of time until deemed adequate to the complexity of the mystery.

Influences on Later Times

The seriousness of the training was often underlined with vows of secrecy, and penalties for breaking it. The penalty of death was not unusual, and some think the breaking of the code may have been contributed to the deaths of Socrates and Christ.

Having attained that insight leaves open few portals:
- guild
- literary
  - Hesiod - Works and Days
  - Old Testament - Book of Job
  - Mozart - Illuminati (*The Magic Flute*, an opera including Masonic rituals and beliefs, was the last opera he wrote)
  - Kubrick - Illuminati (many if not all of his films—including *The Shining*, *2001*, and *A Clockwork Orange*—are full of Illuminati symbols. *Eyes Wide Shut*, the phrase itself, is a calling card among secret societies, meaning 'my eyes are shut to your misdeeds, brother.' This anonymity is required of the participants, otherwise the society's moneyed elite would be revealed. He died only days after submitting the first cut of the film to Warner Brothers.)
- teaching
  - Parables
  - Delphic
  - Mullah Nasrudin Tales
  - Aesop's Fables
- governance
  - Saducee/Pharisee conflict of Christ's day was a target of Jesus' wrath, making their lack of support for him understandable.

- Nimrod
  - great warrior in ancient Babylon established a religious system, based upon witchcraft and idolatry, as an "alternative" to the predominant monotheistic form.
  - Soon after, Shem, one of Noah's sons, militarily attacked, defeated, and executed Nimrod and many of his Satanic priests and followers.
  - The Babylon Mysteries then spread to Egypt, where the story of the death of Nimrod and Shem's dismemberment of his body was retold as the story of Osiris. Most of the key legends of which the occult Mysteries are comprised have been retold in many cultures and always with names and places unique to the specific culture.
- Black Hand (unification of South Slavs) responsible for assassination of Archduke Ferdinand (heir apparent Austro Hungary) leading to WW I
- National Security
  - ambiguity
  - necessity
- Secret Societies

"Commerce, empires and universal religions eventually brought virtually every Sapiens on every continent into the global world we live in today." [HARARI]

~Notes~

---

[38] Not to be confused with Ethnology. The roots of the two words are ethic (moral) vs.ethnic (cultural)

Gaining Knowledge
[from pp. 7, 22, 30, 44]

The study of *knowledge and its acquisition* is called epistemology. The pivotal concepts, *know* and *learn*, form the root verbs. See section [CONFUSING CONCEPTS *ii*] and Notes [GRAMMAR]. In the West, Pythagorus seems to have begun with epistemology, starting with concrete sensory information. He soon used abstract aspects of that information, expanded into theoretical facets of mathematics and spreading to observations of the relationship of pitch to the length of the string on an instrument.

> "...occasionally Pythagoras draws on the theory of music, and designates the distance between the Earth and the Moon as a whole tone, that between the Moon and Mercury as a semitone, ... the seven tones thus producing the so-called diapason, *i.e..* a universal harmony".
>
> [PLINY THE ELDER]

The effort seems to have expanded as the community of Pythagoreans incorporated his precepts and axioms into their life-style to the point that modern Westerners would have trouble discriminating them from a modern cult. It reached a plateau with the disagreement between two of the prominent thinkers of historical times, Plato and Aristotle:

Plato and Aristotle seemed to agree on external reality, but disagreed on the role of experience in learning [AUNE]:

- Plato - knowledge by reason alone is superior to that by sense experience (Rationalism)
- Aristotle - knowledge can only be gained, *if at all*, by experience. (Empiricism).

"Aristotle considered the most fundamental features of reality in the twelve books of the *Metaphysics*...Plato got bogged down in the theory of forms." [KEMERLING Aristotle]

The Church Fathers in Medieval times tended to follow Aristotle, but used Plato as a template for doctrinal declarations.

This abridged version of classical Greek epistemology seems to be the tool kit most Western thinkers use. Neither side does justice to the originators, but helps explain from where the Western attitudes in religion and science got their platform. A look to East thought will track the origins of some of this thinking, and fill in gaps.

Knowledge is acquired, in the Eastern (Hindu) view [STEVKO 2014], according to the Vedas [WITZEL], by the individual spirit, which is formed when an individual consciousness (soul) attaches to and activates the individual primordial materiality (body). The individual spirit evolves (which is the purpose of the union) to a state with no equivalent in English, but in Sanskrit is called *awakened intelligence*. The designation refers to its characteristics of intelligence and luminosity, and to its function, comparable to our definition of perception as the processing of the elements of knowledge. This state is possibly confused with consciousness, because of the similarity of function, and because at this stage, much of consciousness is not yet evolved, and this stage is simply a step in the evolution to higher consciousness. The distinction is important because awakened intelligence must remain active for the process of evolution to continue to higher states. It is akin to a Western person who is spiritually invested to confuse enhanced perceptive abilities with understanding.

There does seem to be a preference in the East to consider knowledge acquisition as part of spiritual development; whereas the attitude in the West does seem more pragmatic. The Western pragmatism does seem to have replaced spiritual development by embedding organized religion into culture as validator of morals.

Inquiries on how to gain knowledge tend to fall into a briar patch of words: experience, reason, sensory, innate, empirical, rational, phenomenal, noumenal. If matched as dichotomous pairs, one pole of which can be construed to form a loose synonym family:

knowledge	external	internal
method of processing	experience	reason
route of data entry	sensory	innate
name of process	empirical	rational
type of information	phenomenal	noumenal

The development of these pairs seems to have happened in concert with the accepted meaning of the word at the time in history that the words were coined. At each level the conceiver of the notion tries to describe the notion so it can be broadly accepted as an explanation for the time, and illuminate concepts leading to it, which are vague. The expectation is that it will reach forward to inspire and to invest subsequent ideas. As the then modern concept is widely accepted, that application of new knowledge will, in turn, influence the change in meaning of earlier concepts. In plain language, what is suggested here leans toward the view that the more other original thinkers will contemplate (speculate/ deliberate) the array of ideas related to their thesis, and formulate rigorously a conclusion deliberated in good faith, based on preceding ideas, and annealed in public dialectic. At each cycle, the framer feels that there are nuances that need its own referent label, and the synonym list multiplies. As notions connected to past ideas are formulated, so the vocabulary of the past is modified, enlarged, and change in concert with the new idea. The old vocabulary is never quite cleaned up, as the original meanings of the words may be the only clue to to the original meaning of the concept. The canon of works held in the discipline of Philosophy is therefore ever changing in meaning, as each work is refreshed in a new context.

None of the Socratics were able to prove any of their assertions. It was a topic of great concern to them. Socrates is quoted by [PLATO*Phaedo*] as having offered three arguments for the immortality of the soul; and further introduces the concept of *Justified True Belief* in [PLATO *Theaetetus*]. Then, [ARISTOTLE *Organon*] established the standard for Logic as it was understood in the Western world for almost two millennia.

The verification for their claims was threefold: 1. internally, they accepted intuitive recognition of the truth, as suggested by Socrates [PLATO *Meno*], and by [DIOGENES LAERTIUS]; 2. externally, their dialectic was honed in debate, well enough to not need further fixing; 3. the more objective the description of a concept is, the more likely it is to be accepted as real.

Returning to plain talk - it is as though Socrates, Plato, and Aristotle's formulation had been not just innovated, but discovered as an imperishable permanent revelation. Indeed, they had impressive resourcefulness, but no abilities that we do not have. The world around them, barring what is called progress, is the same world that surrounds us. Tangible objects were there for their use, just as they clutter our lives. As children they had to develop a denotative vocabulary in common with their community, just as we need to discriminate grape vines from poison ivy.

Perhaps the reason *the European philosophical tradition ... consists of a series of footnotes to Plato* [WHITEHEAD] may be that the cultural belief system, the conventional wisdom, the popular notions of the time have not been sufficiently updated enough to demand a restructuring of what have become edicts; and the vocabulary of the time did not reflect clearly enough what would otherwise have served as more transparent interpretations, and have become imbedded in the canon, flattening the original meaning.

Specifically, the modern concept of *perception* has not yet reached broad acceptance beyond academic cognitive psychology to mean 'processing in the brain of input stimuli' rather than still being read as an adequate synonym for sensation or awareness. Plato clearly understood that sensory information was processed at a level higher than simple awareness: "...I mean the conversation which the soul holds with herself."[PLATO Theaetetus].

Hume's idea of outward and inward impressions is similar to Locke's theory of simple and complex ideas. These reflect almost identically to the sensation/ perception analogy.

Kant sets a totally unique stage for the reception that has yet to be perceived in the caesura between perception - reflection and creativity.

The biological contribution to discrimination, evaluation, verification is not usually considered a philosophical aspect, but is of such immense importance in the development of cognition and the very genesis of philosophy as a distinct manner of thought, that ignoring it at this junction risks perilous conclusions. The aversion to science as having privileged access to knowledge (Scientism) is important, but should not allow philosophy to ignore, or even spurn its offspring, science, from deliberations.

SENSORY EXPERIENCE / INNATE KNOWLEDGE

In the debate about whether knowledge is acquired entirely by experience or is entirely innate, we could propose a thought experiment in which there are two hypothetical groups of animals:

Group 1 acquires knowledge entirely by experience -> spends more time on trial and error learning -> improvises more easily in an unstable or changing environment.

Group 2 relies entirely on innate knowledge (instinct or intuition.[39]) ->
performs more efficiently due to the knowledge possessed->
in an unstable or changing environment, would be disadvantaged.

= = = =

---

[39] The notions of instinct and intuition are more complex than they appear, and on closer examination will both reveal reliance on innateness and experience. This topic is beyond the scope of this work.

GRAMMAR [from pp. 16, 102]

In elementary grammar, verbs are called action words; but in more complex discourse, there are subgroups of action (direction, time) that the verb is capable of discriminating:

- voice [O.E.D.]- indicates the direction of the activity:
  - active - the <u>subject</u> of the verb does the action.
  - passive - the <u>object</u> of the verb is acted upon.
- tense - marks the flow of time:
  - past
  - present
  - future
- aspect - marks the duration of time:
  - a <u>stative verb</u> describes a *state of being*, static or unchanging over time.
  - a <u>dynamic verb</u> which describes an action, a process that changes over time.

These differences are refined by [BINNICK 1991] and by [KOLLN 1998]. Kolln further suggests that we think of the difference between stative and dynamic in terms of *willed* and *unwilled* qualities.

The difference in activity, if not mined, leads to mis-understanding [CONFUSING CONCEPTS *ii* learn/know]. Learning is different than knowing and represents not only a different activity, but implies possession where desire is the actual activity.

In addition there are multiple forms of the verb (base auxiliary), further extending subtlty of meaning extending to: **Tense–aspect–mood** The <u>grammatical system</u> of a language that covers the expression of <u>tense</u> (location in time), <u>aspect</u> (fabric of time – a single block of time, continuous flow of time, or repetitive occurrence), and <u>mood</u> or <u>modality</u> (degree of necessity, obligation, probability, ability).[BYBEE]

= = = =

DIKW [from p. 17]
(Data - Information - Knowledge - Wisdom)

"According to Russell Ackoff, a systems theorist and professor of organizational change, the content of the human mind can be classified into five categories:

1   Data: symbols
2   Information: data that are processed to be useful; provides answers to "who", "what", "where", and "when" questions
3   Knowledge: application of data and information; answers "how" questions
4   Understanding: appreciation of "why"
5   Wisdom: evaluated understanding.

Ackoff indicates that the first four categories relate to the past; they deal with what has been or what is known. Only the fifth category, wisdom, deals with the future because it incorporates vision and design. With wisdom, people can create the future rather than just grasp the present and past. But achieving wisdom isn't easy; people must move successively through the other categories." [BELLINGER]

An Antithetical View

ABSTRACT "The now taken-for-granted notion that data lead to information, which leads to knowledge, which in turn leads to wisdom was first specified in detail by R. L. Ackoff in 1988. The Data-Information-Knowledge-Wisdom hierarchy is based on filtration, reduction, and transformation. Besides being causal and hierarchical, the scheme is pyramidal, in that data are plentiful while wisdom is almost nonexistent. Ackoff's formula linking these terms together this way permits us to ask what the *opposite* of knowledge is and whether analogous principles of hierarchy, process, and pyramiding apply to it. The inversion of the Data-Information-Knowledge-Wisdom hierarchy produces a series of opposing terms (including misinformation, error, ignorance, and stupidity) but not exactly a chain or a pyramid. Examining the connections between these phenomena contributes to our understanding of the contours and limits of knowledge." [BERNSTEIN]

Alternatives to learning hierarchies, processes and antithetical views have been previously reviewed [Stevko 2013 *Mental Functioning*].

====

Before there was anything particular, the Universe was a primordial disorganized void, the personification of which was Chaos.

Out of Chaos emerged The first primordial deities:

Entity	Personification (deity)
earth	Gaea
underworld	Tartarus
sky	Uranus
love	Eros
darkness	Erebus
night	Nyx

The primordial deities Gaia and Uranus give birth to the Titans.

The Titan gods Cronus and Rhea give birth to the Olympians.

The Olympians, Zeus, Poseidon, Hades, Hestia, Hera and Demeter overthrew the Titans. The warring of the gods ends with the reign of Zeus.

When Cronus rebelled against his father, Uranus, and castrated him. The blood which fell to earth generated a race of Giants. They were not outsized, but strong and aggressive.

Other fabulous races also arose, the origin of which Hesiod does not explain:
- the Telchines - magician-smiths and sea daimones invented the art of metal-working. In myth, roles almost identical to other fabulous beings.
- the Cyclopes - member of a primordial race of giants (not Giants), each with a single eye in the middle of his forehead
- the Dactyls - ancient smiths and healing magicians. In some myths, they are associated with the Great Mother; in others, Hephaestus' employ
- the Korybantes - the armed and crested ecstatic dancers. Cabiri an offshoot of this race.
- the Kuretes- rhythmic dancers employed first as distraction, then incorporated in ritual.

It is well to note that other races with supernatural connections arose within other cultures, mythic systems and established religions, e.g., Norse dwarfs, Celtic leprechauns, Canaanite angels, etc.

= = = =

Mystery - The Hanged Man
[from pp. 76, 91, 119]
Origin - Tarot card

Characters:	Principle:
traitors of old (sacrifice self for a cause)	see things from an "inverted" perspective
babe in womb	hangs suspended between one world and the next
Odin	allows himself to be hung so as to gain wisdom for the world.

Narrative: Man suspended from a tree in the inverted position by one leg. Other limbs free. Position relaxed. Face not contorted.

Explanation:
Whether or not you subscribe to psychic readings, the explanation in Tarot card #12, The Hanged Man, gives an excellent example of the use of representation in mythic motifs. The suspended man has reached a crossroads or paradox that has been thoroughly explored without satisfactory resolution and has willingly allowed his position to be suspended and to be placed in a unique position in order to attain a new perspective on the conundrum.

The willingness involves sacrifice, as in [Odin Mysteries] giving an eye to be able to drink from the font of knowledge held by his nemesis; or as in Husserl holding an apparently essential component of an incongruous concept in abeyance, while continuing to explore other apparently essential components until a fit becomes obvious. Surely, a form of meditation or reflection.

Giving up an eye may seem hyperbolic; but in surrender (a part of willing suspension), something is always given up, perhaps only the pride of a prime position; but, in the end the one suspended is never again the same - a NEW man. The upright card (inverted man) represents suspension; the reversed card (upright man) represents martyrdom. [NICHOLS] [MELETINSKY]

An Interpretation
"Esoterically, the Hanged Man is the human spirit which is suspended from heaven by a single thread. Wisdom, not death, is the reward for this voluntary sacrifice during which the human soul, suspended above the world of illusion, and meditating upon its unreality, is rewarded by the achievement of self-realization." [HALL]

====

Reification [from pp. 32, 96,]

reification
- treating an abstraction as a concrete thing
- make an object out of any abstract thing.

objectification
- present as an object
- to represent concretely

deification
- personify as a deity

Personification
- treats anything (abstract or concrete) as though it has human qualities
- allows you to attach human qualities to anything (abstract or not)

= = = =

Prejudice in Learning [from p. 30]

The gap between <u>innate knowledge</u> and <u>knowledge by experience</u> is confounded not so much by animosity of the originators, Plato and Aristotle, who were not so much adversarial personally, but were more concerned about the basic understanding that they did share [GERSON]. They were working different sides of the same street, as are modern troubadours[40]. They each, like many modern scholars held views that are both aporetic (a disbelieving attitude) and doctrinal (the results of their speculation) [CICERO]. It was later proponents who rigidified their speculations from doctrine to dogma and have defensively built entire belief systems into the fabric of the way of life. As so often happens in the construction of belief systems, the notions become embedded in such a way that parsing individual aspects, for their contribution to meaning, is no longer possible without dismantling support structures that are no longer necessary. The learners, then, find new data not only incorporable into into new concepts, but need to deconstruct older concepts to find if the speculation can be helpful in unique conceptualizations. A child, then, who was raised believing that the justification for a moral life is reward on a metaphysical plane, is not even available to participate in honest dialectic about physics, unless its outer parameters are restricted from the discussion. That child's ability to learn is prejudiced. He needs to not only consider justification as a thing in itself, but as a power that could endanger the

---

[40] Craig [WERNER] - re: Jerry Lee Lewis and Little Richard.
    Josh White - re: Hank Williams and himself. [personal communication]

foundations of his personality. Plato offers a dilemma of just this sort in the Republic under a discussion of justice. [Notes^{Justice}]

Dealing with prejudiced learning: The information we learn may have been corrupted by many factors:
- the information may not reflect what we think it does. A rock is a rock and we can certify that belief by testing it. An offense we feel when someone provokes us may as likely be their slight as easily as it could be our sensitivity.
- our sensory organs are constructed of fallible material and may sense phenomena incorrectly.
- the processing of the data acquired may be deficient due to a number of missing factors.
- as we progress toward our prime, many of the things we believe may have been accepted under the assurance of folk wisdom.

The acquired knowledge that is corrupt, prejudiced, or simply mistaken will repeatedly run into mismatches in our perceptive system. In addition, that system has a constant weather reporter called the emotions that warn us of incorrect information that is contaminating our systems. These systems are self corrective, given a chance. Most religions provide curative elements, e.g., prayer, meditation: see [NOTES $^{Hanged\ Man}$]. Unfortunately, organized religion has usurped those elements into their rituals, which are already so dogma strewn that the form of the elements has become more ritual than curative. In any debate a discussant may be prejudiced for or against some principles in the argument, even before beginning; at the risk of bolstering or losing foundational ground.

= = = =

Biographies of Ancient Thinkers [from pp. 22, 45]

Among the earliest historians to mention secret societies, were:

- Aeschylus c. 525 - c.455 BC
- Herodotus c. 484 - 425 BC
- Strabo c.64 BC - c. AD 24
- Pausanias c. AD 110 - c. 180

Others have been implicated:

> "Socrates refused to be initiated into the Eleusinian Mysteries, for knowing its principles without being a member of the order he realized that membership would seal his tongue." [Hall]

> "Would Pindar, Plato, Cicero, Epictetus, have spoken of them with such admiration, if the hierophant had satisfied himself with loudly proclaiming his own opinions, or those of his order?" [Ouvaroff]

> "Socrates is described as a revealer of these Mysteries in Phaedrus. This may have been the basis of the indictment of "impiety" that led to his execution." [SWANSON]

Socrates' initiation into a mystery society is suggested by [HALL]. [PLATO Meno] describes a conversation between Socrates and an Athenian intellectual named Meno. In this work the method of acquiring virtue is discussed and the conclusion is ambiguous. Socrates tells Meno that if he wants a true and deep understanding of the meaning of virtue, he should accompany him to the Mysteries and be initiated. Other interpreters say he refused initiation because the vow of secrecy would restrict his philosophical investigations.

[Plato ^{Phaedo}] seems to have come closer than any to connecting the Mysteries with Socrates; being almost a handbook of mysteries in the form of dualities as understood in Western thinking.

Plato understood that real philosophy was discovered in living the truth, not in reading about it; and for that reason he adamantly proclaimed he had never written down his ultimate teaching. [BOSWORTH]

> "Those who have not the true philosophic temper, but a mere surface coloring of opinions penetrating, like sunburn, only skin deep, when they see how great the range of studies is, how much labour is involved in it, and how necessary to the pursuit it is to have an orderly regulation of the daily life, come to the conclusion that the thing is difficult and impossible for them, and are actually incapable of carrying out the course of study; while some of them persuade themselves that they have sufficiently studied the whole matter and have no need of any further effort. This is the sure test and is the safest one to apply to those who live in luxury and are incapable of continuous effort; it ensures that such a man shall not throw the blame upon his teacher but on himself, because he cannot bring to the pursuit all the qualities necessary to it.
> ...There neither is nor ever will be a treatise of mine on the subject. For it does not admit of exposition like other branches of knowledge; but after much converse about the matter itself and a life lived together, suddenly a light, as it were, is kindled in one soul by a flame that leaps to it from another,

and thereafter sustains itself. ... But I do not think it a good thing for men that there should be a disquisition, as it is called, on this topic-except for some few, who are able with a little teaching to find it out for themselves. As for the rest, it would fill some of them quite illogically with a mistaken feeling of contempt, and others with lofty and vain-glorious expectations, as though they had learnt something high and mighty." [PLATO *SEVENTH*]

Dialectic (Gk. *dialektos*) refers to reciprocal interchange between persons *or* between *aspects of a person*. One of the extraordinary elements Plato introduces is locating dialectic both in outer discourse and in inner dialogue. [LIVERGOOD]

"a dialogue which the soul has with itself about the objects under its consideration. . . It seems to me that the soul when it thinks is simply engaging in dialectic with itself in which it asks itself questions and answers them itself, affirms and denies. And when it arrives at something definite, either by a gradual process or a sudden leap, when it affirms one thing consistently and without divided counsel, we call this its judgment. So, in my view, to judge is to make a statement, and a judgment is a statement which is not addressed to another person or spoken aloud, but silently addressed to oneself." [PLATO *THEAETETUS*]

"Socrates: I mean the conversation which the soul holds with herself in considering of anything. I speak of what I scarcely understand; but the soul when thinking appears to me to be just talking— asking questions of herself and answering them, affirming and denying. And when she has arrived at a decision, either gradually or by a sudden impulse, and has at last agreed, and does not doubt, this is called her opinion. I say, then, that to form an opinion is to speak, and opinion is a word spoken, —I mean, to oneself and in silence, not aloud or to another: What think you?" [PLATO *Theaetetus J*]

"Therefore every man of worth, when dealing with matters of worth, will be far from exposing them to ill feeling and misunderstanding among men by committing them to writing. In one word, then, it may be known from this that, if one sees written treatises composed by anyone, either the laws of a lawgiver, or in any other form whatever, these are not for that man the things of most worth, if he is a man of worth, but that his treasures are laid up in the fairest spot that he possesses. But if these things were worked at by him as things of real worth, and committed to writing, then surely, not gods, but men "have themselves bereft him of his wits." [PLATO *SEVENTH*]

Many of what [Aristotle *Physics*] referred to as "so-called unwritten doctrines" may have simply been oral teachings that Plato also hold as a primary form of philosophizing.

Plato theorized that ultimate reality is only knowable through reason and reflection, locating it in ideas or eternal forms. Aristotle differed; theorizing ultimate reality is knowable through experience, residing in physical objects, and his writings were often based on first-hand observation.(compare to emergence of mystery religions)

= = = =

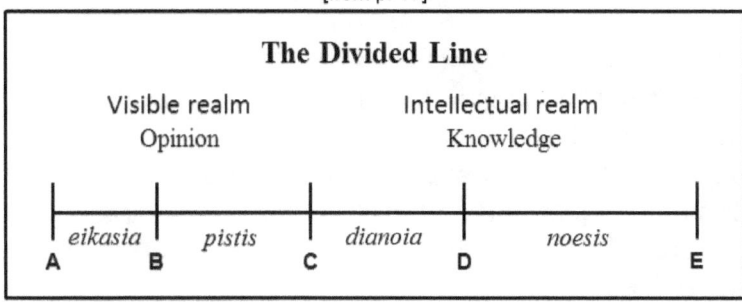

[from p. 17]

The Divided Line

Visible realm   Intellectual realm
Opinion   Knowledge

eikasia   pistis   dianoia   noesis
A   B   C   D   E

- ∘ *eikasia* (delusion or sheer conjecture)
- ∘ *pistis* (belief or confidence)
- ∘ *dianoia* (discursive thought)
- ∘ *noesis* (immediate intuition, apprehension, or mental 'seeing' of principles)

= = = =

JUSTICE [from p. 119]

[PLATO]'s four different views on "What is justice?"
I. Cephalus: Justice is "speaking the truth and paying whatever debts one has incurred."
objection of Socrates: doing these things is sometimes just and sometimes unjust. Example: give weapons back / tell the whole truth to someone who is out of his mind.

II. Polemarchus: justice is "to give each what is owed to him." "justice ... gives benefits to friends and does harm to enemies."
objection of Socrates: "it isn't the function of a just person to harm a friend or anyone else, rather it is the function of his opposite, an unjust person."

III. Thrasymachus: "justice is nothing other than the advantage of the stronger."
objection of Socrates: "no one in any position of rule, insofar as he is a ruler, seeks or orders what is advantageous to himself, but what is advantageous to his subjects."

IV. Glaucon: argues we are only moral because, it pays us or we have to be (later to be known as a social contract theory).

Socrates: "[J]ustice is virtue and wisdom and ... injustice is vice and ignorance" (350*d*).
"[T]hose who are all bad and completely unjust are completely incapable of accomplishing anything." (352*c*)
"[A] just soul and a just man will live well, and an

unjust one badly ... a just person is happy, and an unjust person wretched."

Plato: most treated justice as something external. "Justice is, for Plato, at once a part of human virtue and the bond, which joins man together in society. It is the identical quality that makes good and social . Justice is an order and duty of the parts of the soul, it is to the soul as health is to the body. Plato says that justice is not mere strength, but it is a harmonious strength. Justice is not the right of the stronger but the effective harmony of the whole. All moral conceptions revolve about the good of the whole-individual as well as social." [BHANDARI]

= = = =

Experience [from pp. 13, 18, 24, 31-32, 43-46]

"I should write a book," is frequently exclamation by someone who has just had an unusual experience. It takes on additional emphasis if that experience is an instantiation of a meaningful principle, which has been repeated in many variations over a period of time, giving the speaker a cache of expertise, from which others, presumably readers, could gain benefit.

Experience from which one can learn seems to be a hallmark of human bonding. Not only are prehistoric hominid traditions implied in early historic narratives, but animal socialization is replete with examples of transferred learning.[41] Whether or not these are long-term changes of behavior as a result of individual experience is still being studied. [BOAKES] [HALLIDAY AND SLATER] [HINDE] [STADDON] [McFARLAND]. The consideration of learning has undergone many changes in history. Before Socrates, who was the linchpin of western thought, there had been similar ideas propounded by Pythagoras, who noted the harmonies that held among the sides of a right triangle as well as among the pitches of notes an the length of an instrument's strings. That these harmonies reflected the ultimate nature of reality and was connected with such notions as the immortality of the soul and reincarnation, was connected to folk wisdom and religious ideas in ancient Egypt and pre-Vedic India.

The history of thought, since classical times, seems to imply no limit to the acquisition of knowledge. The

---

[41] tool use to crack open shells and nuts, pack hunting, bee dancing, ant tracking.

expansion of science (original meaning: *scientia* - knowledge), followed by the expansion of natural sciences in Medieval times, followed by general knowledge in the Enlightenment and ultimately the physical sciences in the Scientific Revolution, that almost seems to be a truism...but the premise of which we speak is *learning by experience*. At the beginning of recorded rumination, two of the most prominent thinkers disagreed on that very point, and subsequent thinkers have weighed in on the disagreement, and though much light has been shed on the topic, so has a lot of heat and a lot of defensible positions, embedding the issue so deeply into conventional wisdom that it seems to be an innate truth.

That the aggregation of facts we have learned is sometimes called knowledge[42]; and that what we have yet to learn is called The Unknown. There are those who hold that things beyond that are Unknowable, a speculative category that can neither be proved nor disproved at this time. The vastness of the Universe and the ineffability of describing transcendent phenomena certainly makes such claims seem plausible. On the other hand, the rate at which our sensory limitations have been augmented by auxiliary devices and the possibility of solving the mind-body dilemma to enhance understanding of what are now called metaphysical phenomena offers hope that the word *possibility*, earlier in this line, can be comfortably changed to *probability*.

= = = =

---

[42] Learning and Knowledge are sometimes used as synonyms. To clarify, see Notes Gaining Knowledge

CLASSIFICATION [from p. 25]

classification - The action or process of arranging things or
     sets according to shared qualities or characteristics.
discrimination - Recognition and understanding of the
     difference between one thing and another,

Taxonomy[43] is the classification of living beings
     (originally), by characteristics[44].
Typology is the classification of any things by shared
     characteristics (types)[45].
Topology is the classification of things by surface
     appearance[46].

Something rather than Nothing

The different categories of *Classification* can be
abstracted into an axiom: Classification is thinking. As
has been pointed out in LEARNING PROCESS IN ACTION,
awareness leads to stimulation, then to perception,
which, in placing objects perceived into memory, is
actually performing what could be called a
classification function in information technology and
psychology. The fact that two objects appear *same* in

---

[43] Gk. *taxis* ('order', 'arrangement') and *nomos* ('law' or 'science')

[44] The branch of science concerned with classification, especially
of organisms (*Biology*); systematics (classification and
nomenclature).When the characteristic of sensation is used as a
discriminating point, the beings we have categorized as animals
have sensory systems similar to ours; those called plants have a
sensory system quite different; and the inanimate objects do not
have a sensory system by the definition now in use - though a
re-categorization of the definition (as in Animism or Poetry) can
change that.

[45] esp. archaeology, linguistics.

[46] esp. anatomy, geography, and sometimes in social sciences.

consciousness causes so little activity in the nervous system, contrary to when two objects are different, that rings a dis-chord in the mind, resulting in disturbed harmony, unbalanced equilibrium, a state which in the physiologic sphere is called homeostasis. [CANNON, W.] This state, chemically, is known by all scientists and apprehended to the extent that predictions could be based on it. The degree of understanding, profound as it seems to the uneducated, is no more deeply understood than the nature of gravity, or any other important concept (love, faith, patriotism, humanity).

When the homeostasis is disrupted, if the concept we have is adequate for practical purposes, we can ignore the disturbing factor without untoward consequences...seemingly. In fact, the only way we can apparently ignore sensory data is when it is close enough to former data to be recognized as having been placed into memory. Good enough is good enough...for homeostasis.

What is called understanding of topics, be they physical or mental, is an accumulation of facts. Those facts relate one to the other, first in way of similarity or contiguity. That is a function of perception. Then they are related, imaginatively and tentatively, in ever more complicated ways. As a result, consciousness accepts that is *good enough* to get things done. The concept resolves obscure inconsistencies at a level that the concept, itself, is no longer held as incongruous. This represents understanding basic enough to pass for Truth. We all have learned to work with that level of understanding as being *good enough*, pragmatically. It gets things done. Even the concept of good enough is modified when the goal is discrimination.

Nothing rather than Something

It's difficult to imagine Nothing. Infants work so hard building the biological stratum that keeps the usual things in place around us; or to notice when they're not there. Though it's neurologically complex to mentally build and hold a model of the Usual, it takes even more psychological peregrinations to notice that sometimes a Usual object is gone; and it also takes exquisitely intricate circuitry, prodigious memory and manipulative ability to be able to conceive that the absent thing has gone somewhere.

Gone somewhere? The mental placeholder for a place of choice is usually the more attractive of the two basic emotions - Pleasure / Pain (the other emotions can be considered progeny). So if the thing has gone away, it must be in a place from which I can retrieve it at will. Option: it's down the River Styx, a place of unlikely return. To even be capable of conceiving a place that is not here requires a capacity reserved for those having reached the age of reason.

Not Here. Let's call the place the Unknown. Both the hidden and the unknowable are reifications of the unknown. The primary business of modern seekers is to make known the unknown (by the techniques of their trade). When one is assured that the information in question is verified, then information that is held as hidden is just an annoyance. The Unknowable is usually considered to hold the Unknown, and presents a challenge to further exploration. How much of the Unknowable is available to the seeker is a matter of faith. That border, between the Unknown and the Unknowable, might be more flexible than we thought; considering its fluctuation on the basis of the revolutions in thinking by Copernicus, Kant, Darwin, Freud, and possibly Bohr/Einstein. Each of those revolutions has changed what were considered unshakable assumptions of the time.

And yet, to stand on an isolated summit and scan the canopy of stars, an honest visceral response is to feel the relative difference, reflected in:

- [Kant 1785] declared that only two things inspire genuine awe: "the starry sky above and the moral law within".
- Breton Fisherman's Prayer - *Thy sea is so great, My boat so small.* The common, but inauthentic response is to claim 'insignificance'. I call that inauthentic because, though it may reflect the relative difference, it couches it in negative psychological terms.
- Anything much bigger than us can make us feel small, but it needn't. A preadolescent boy, visiting the Grand Canyon, said, "If they would let me get closer to the edge, I could spit a mile." He did not let the size make him feel insignificant. Realists know they'll never know everything, but are not intimidated into thinking anything is unknowable.
- Like the Medieval Alchemists, they realize changing lead into gold is not feasible, but they continued the quest and came up with modern chemistry. Even the Breton fisherman would feel insignificance only at the risk of not returning to port.

= = = =

ETHOLOGY[47]

1a branch of knowledge dealing with human
character and with its formation and evolution
2 the scientific and objective study of animal
behavior especially under natural conditions [MW]

A social science providing a much needed fill to a gap
in behavioral studies. We pointed out, in Confusing
Concepts i, that secret societies and group secrets
are incongruous. The notion of *secret* is <u>not sharing</u>;
the notion of *group* and *society* is <u>sharing</u>. Creation
AND resolution of this conundrum lies in human
behavior. So it seems fitting to close with a nod
towards the evolution of Ethology, the study of human
character and behavior.

Aristotle (384-322) BC
• Basic Idea - *scala naturae* living beings were classified on an ideal pyramid representing the simplest
  animals on the lower levels, with complexity increasing progressively toward the top, occupied by
  human beings.
• Expanded Idea - In the Western world of the time,
  people believed animal species were eternal and
  immutable, created with a specific purpose, as this
  seemed the only possible explanation for the
  incredible variety of living beings and their surprising
  adaptation to their habitats.

Jean-Baptiste Lamarck (1744 - 1829)
• His theory substantially comprised two statements:
  1. animal organs and behavior can change
     according to the way they are used

---

[47] Not to be confused with Ethnology. The roots of the two words
are ethic (moral) vs.ethnic (cultural)

2. those characteristics can transmit from one generation to the next
- When Charles Darwin went to the Galapagos Islands, he was well aware of Lamarck's theories and was influenced by them.

Charles Darwin (1809-1882)
- Ethology as a topic of biology, leads to particular concern:
  - evolution of behavior
  - understanding of behavior in terms of the theory of natural selection.
- In one sense, the first modern ethologist was [Darwin ^{Expression}], whose book *The Expression of the Emotions in Man and Animals* influenced many ethologists. He pursued his interest in behavior by encouraging his.

George Romanes (1848-1894)
- Darwin's protégé
- investigated animal learning and intelligence using an anthropomorphic method, anecdotal cognitivism, that did not gain scientific support
- initiated Neo-Darwinism and Comparative Psychology

Oskar Heinroth (1871-1945)
- rediscovered imprinting

Julian Huxley (1887-1975)
- concentrated on behaviors called instinctive, or natural, in that they occur in all members of a species under specified circumstances.
- Their beginning for studying the behavior of a new species was to construct an **ethogram** (a description of the main types of behavior with their frequencies of occurrence). This provided an

objective, cumulative data-base of behavior, which subsequent researchers could check and supplement.

John H. Crook (1930 -2011)
- distinguished comparative ethology from social ethology
- comparative ethology: examining animals as individuals
- social ethology: behavior of social groups of animals and the social structure within them.

Robert Ardrey (1908 -1980)
- *The Social Contract: A Personal Inquiry into the Evolutionary Sources of Order and Disorder* was published in 1970.
- Considered animal behavior and human behavior to be comparable phenomena.

E. O. Wilson (1929 -)
- *Sociobiology: The New Synthesis* appeared in 1975, and since that time, the study of behavior has been much more concerned with social aspects. It has also been driven by the stronger, but more sophisticated, Darwinism associated with Wilson, Robert Trivers, Crook and William Hamilton.
- behavioral ecology (a related development) has also helped transform ethology. Furthermore, a substantial rapprochement with comparative psychology has occurred, so the modern scientific study of behavior offers a more or less seamless spectrum of approaches: from animal cognition to more traditional comparative psychology, ethology, sociobiology, and behavioral ecology. Sociobiology has more recently developed into evolutionary psychology.

Bibliography

Abbott, B. P. et al. (LIGO Scientific Collaboration and Virgo Collaboration)*Observation of Gravitational Waves from a Binary Black Hole Merger. Physical Review Letters* 116 (6). (2016)

Ackoff, R. L., *From Data to Wisdom*, Journal of Applied Systems Analysis, Volume 16, 1989 p 3-9.

Adelman, K., *Secrets and Mysteries*, NPR commentary: All Things Considered: September 18, 2002

Aeschylus *Kabeiroi* (Greek tragedy, now lost).

Anthony, David W. (2010). *The Horse, the Wheel, and Language: How Bronze-Age Riders from the Eurasian Steppes Shaped the Modern World*. Princeton University Press. pp. 134–135.

Apuleius, *Metamorphoses*, or *The Golden Ass*

Aristotle, *Metaphysics*

Aristotle, *Physics*, 209b13–15.

Assmann, Jan (2001) [1984]. *The Search for God in Ancient Egypt*. Translated by David Lorton.

Atsma, A. J., editor, *The Theoi Project : Greek Mythology : Cabeiri*

Aune, B. Rationalism, 1970, *Empiricism, and Pragmatism: An Introduction*. New York: Random House,

Bellinger, Gene. *Systems Thinking* 2004

Bernstein, J.H., *The data-information-knowledge-wisdom hierarchy and its antithesis*, NASKO, 2011

Besant, A., *Zoroastrianism*, Four Great Religions 1897

Bhandari, D.R. *Plato's Concept Of Justice: An Analysis*

Binnick, R. I. 1991. *Time and the Verb: a Guide to Tense and Aspect*. New York: Oxford University Press.

Boakes, R., *From Darwin to Behaviorism: Psychology and the Minds of Animals* (1984).

Bosworth, R., *The Lives of Plato & Socrates*

Boyce, Mary (1979) *Zoroastrians: Their Religious Beliefs and Practices* London: Routledge & Kegan Paul, pp. 27-29

Brentano, F., *Psychology from an Empirical Standpoint*, trans. A.C. Rancurello, D.B. Terrell, L.L. McAlister, London, New York 1995. p. 68.

Britannica Encyclopedia, 9th ed., *Cardinal*

Burkert, Walter (1985). *Greek Religion*, Sect. VI.1.3 "The Kabeiroi and Samothrace",Harvard University Press.

Bybee, Joan L., Revere Perkins, and William Pagliuca (1994) *The Evolution of Grammar: Tense, Aspect, and Modality in the Languages of the World*. University of Chicago Press.

Cannon, W., *The Wisdom of the Body.*

Carr-Gomm, Philip, *Druid Mysteries: Ancient Wisdom for the 21st Century*, Rider, Random House, 2002.

Casavis *The Greek Origins of Freemasonry* p. 111

Castelvecchi, Davide; Witze, Witze . *Einstein's gravitational waves found at last*. Nature News. (February 11, 2016)

Chomsky, N., *Syntactic Structures* (1957), Mouton & Co.
Chomsky, N. (1959). *A Review of B. F. Skinner's Verbal Behavior.* Language **35**(1), pp. 26–58.
Christie, James, *Disquisition on Etruscan Vases,* W. Bulmer for T. Becket, London,1806
Cicero, *Academica* I.17-18
Clement of Alexandria, *Exhortation to the Heathen,* ch. 2.
Delaney, A., 2013 *Empiricism – From Locke to Hume*
Darwin, C., *The Origin of Species* (1859), 104f.
Darwin, C., *The Expression of the Emotions in Man and Animals* (1872)
Descartes, R., 1628, *Rules for the Direction of our Native Intelligence* Rules II and III, pp. 1–4, in *Descartes: Selected Philosophical Writings*: Cambridge University Press, 1988.
Descartes, R. 1647 *Meditations on First Philosophy,* Meditation II, VI
Dewey, J., Bentley, A.F., (1949). *Knowing and the Known.* Boston: Beacon Press. pp. 58, 72–74.
Diogenes Laertius, (Plato's) "Theory of Ideas" in *Lives of Eminent Philosophers*. Book III. Paragraph 15.
Eliot, T.S. (1934) "The Rock", Faber & Faber.
Enslin, Morton Scott (1938) *Christian Beginnings*
Faulkes, Anthony (Trans.) (1995). *Edda.* Everyman.
Frazer, James George (1890). *The Golden Bough.* New York: Touchstone, 1996
Gerson, L. P., *Aristotle and Other Platonists.*, Ithaca: Cornell University Press, 2005
Goethe, W., *Faust,* Walter Kaufman, translator, Random House, New York 1990
Hall, M.P., *The Secret Teachings of all Ages* Philosophical Research Society (1928)
The Mysteries: The First Secret Society
Halliday, T.R. and Slater, P.J.B.(eds.), *Animal Behavior*, vol. 3: *Genes, Development, and Learning* (1983)
Harari, Yuval, Noah, *Sapiens,* p264
Harper, D., *Online Etymological Dictionary*
Heckethorn, C., *The Secret Societies of All Ages & Countries* quoted in Hall, M.P., *The Secret Teachings Of All Ages*
Heinrich, Bernd, *MIND OF THE RAVEN OTHER DETAILS Investigations and Adventures With Wolf-Birds* Cliff Street Books / HarperCollins Publishers
Herodotus, *The Histories (iii. 37)*
Hesiod, *Theogeny*
Hinde, R.A., *Animal Behavior: A Synthesis of Ethology and Comparative Psychology*, 2nd ed. (1970)
Hume, David (1739) *A Treatise of Human Nature*
Hume, David (1748) *An Enquiry Concerning Human Understanding* The Harvard Classics. 1909–14.
Husserl, Edmund, Translated by David Carr as *The Crisis of European Sciences and Transcendental Phenomenology* (Northwestern University Press: Evanston, 1954)

Hutton, Ronald (2009). *Blood and Mistletoe: The History of the Druids in Britain*. New Haven,   Connecticut: Yale University Press.

Juvenal, *Satire X* (10.356)

Janda, M., (2000), *Eleusis: das indogermanische Erbe der Mysterien*, (Habil. Thesis), Innsbruck.

Jaynes, J., *The Origin of Consciousness in the Breakdown of the Bicameral Mind*, Houghton Mifflin   Company, 1976

Jung, C.G., *Symbols of Transformation* 1912

Jung, C.G., *Psychology and Religion: West and East* is Volume 11 in *The Collected Works of C. G. Jung*, Routledge & Kegan Paul p.243 1975

Kant, I., (1781) *Critique of Pure Reason* A256/B312, p. 27

Kant, I., (1783) *Prolegomena to Any Future Metaphysics*

Kant, I., 1785 *Grounding for the Metaphysics of Morals.*

Kemerling, G., *Aristotle: Forms and Souls* in The Philosophy   Pages

Kemerling, Garth, *Locke: The Origin of Ideas* in The Philosophy Pages

Kerényi, C., Manheim R., *Eleusis: Archetypal Image of Mother and Daughter* 1991

KJV - King James Version, *Holy Bible.*

Knoche, Grace F. (1999)*The Mystery Schools* Theosophical University Press.

Kolln, Martha. *Understanding English Grammar*, 5th edition. Macmillan, 1998.

Leeming, D., *The Oxford Companion to World Mythology* (Oxford University Press, 2005), p. 98

Leibniz, W.,H., *Monadology* §§31–32

Livergood, N. D., Inner Dialectic, Hermes Press

Maimonides, Moses. *Guide for the Perplexed* (1904)

Manetho, *The Aegyptiaca,* The earliest surviving attestation in Josephus' *Contra Apionem*

Mark, Joshua J., *Osiris,* Ancient History Encyclopedia, 06 March 2016

McFarland,D., *Animal Behavior: Psychology, Ethology, and Evolution* (1985).

Meletinsky, E.M., *The Poetics of Myth* Routledge 1998 p.290

Mettinger, Tryggve N. D. (2001). *The Riddle of Resurrection: Dying and Rising Gods in the Ancient Near East*. Coniectanea Biblica, Old Testament, 50, Stockholm: Almqvist & Wiksell

Morford, M., Lenardon, R. J., Sham, M. *Classical Mythology*, Chapter 13, Oxford University Press, Tenth   Edition 2013

Moscati, Sabatino. 2001 *The Face of the Ancient Orient*

MW - Merriam-Webster Dictionary knowledge insight, judgement, ethology.

Nichols, Sallie 1980 *Jung and Tarot: An Archetypal Journey*, Weiser Books

Nietzsche, Friedrich, *The Birth of Tragedy* (Trans. Douglas Smith), Oxford University Press, 2008: pp. xxxii, 28, 109, 140.

Noll, K. L., (2007) *Canaanite Religion*, Religion Compass 1 (1), 61–92

NSF - National Science Foundation, *Gravitational waves detected 100 years after Einstein's prediction*

OED - Wisdom - Having or showing experience, knowledge, and good judgment.

OED - voice of the verb

Ouvaroff, M.(1817) *The Mysteries of Eleusis*, Holmes Publishing Group (August 1992)

Pausanias, *Description of Greece 9. 25. 5 - 26. 1*

Pinker, Steven (2003). *The Blank Slate*. Penguin.

Plato, *The Dialogues, Meno*

Plato, *The Dialogues, Phaedo*, 69e–80c

Plato, *The Dialogues, Phaedrus*, pp. 275-277 (trans. Benjamin Jowett, Oxford University Press).

Plato, *The Republic*, Allegory of the Cave

Plato, *The Republic*, Allegory of the Divided line (509d–511e)

Plato, *The Republic*, trans. G. M. A. Grube, revised by C. D. C. Reeve (Indianapolis: Hackett Publishing Company, 1992) 331c-354a

Plato (360 B.C.E) *The Seventh Letter,* Translated by J. Harward

Plato, *The Theaetetus J,* Translated by Benjamin Jowett

Plato *Theaetetus,*[189e-190a]

Plato, *The Timaeus,* Archer-Hind, R. D.. editor, Macmillan and co. London and New York 1888

Pliny the Elder, 77AD. *Natural History*, books I-II, translated by H. Rackham (1938). Harvard University Press.

Plutarch, *Progress in Virtue* 81e

Popper, K., *The Logic of Scientific Discovery* (1934), p. 280

Random House Dictionary, © Random House, Inc. 2014

Reade, W. W., *THE VEIL OF ISIS* or *MYSTERIES OF THE DRUIDS* (1861) Peter Eckler, Publisher 1881

Rice, F. L. *The Skeptic Tank*

Russell, B. 1910. *Knowledge by Acquaintance and Knowledge by Description.*Proceedings of the Aristotelian Society 11, 108-128.

Scriven, M., "The Key Property of Physical Laws – Inaccuracy," in *Current Issues in the Philosophy   of Science – Proceedings of Section L of the American Association for the Advancement of Sciences, 1959*, edited by H. Feigl and G. Maxwell, (New York: Holt Rinehart and Winston), 1961, pp. 91-104.

Shakespeare, as Brutus, *Julius Caesar* IV.iii

Schryer, J., *Mythological Studies and Depth Psychology*

Staddon, J.E.R., *Adaptive Behavior and Learning* (1983)

Stevko, R., 2013 *Mental Functioning* Graven Image

Stevko, R., 2013 *Shades of Meaning,* Graven Image

Stevko, R., 2014 *Before Philosophy,* Graven Image

Surratt CK, Persico AM, Yang XD, Edgar SR, Bird GS, Hawkins AL, Griffin CA, Li X, Jabs EW, Uhl GR (March 1993). *A human synaptic vesicle monoamine transporter cDNA predicts posttranslational modifications, reveals chromosome 10 gene localization and identifies TaqI RFLPs*. FEBS Lett. 318 (3): 325–30.

Swanson, T., *Metanoia And the Mysteries*

Synesius, *Dio* (1133)

The New Encyclopaedia Britannica, *Sarapis*. Chicago: 15th edn., 1992, Vol. 10, p. 447.

Thompson, S., *Motif-Index of Folk-Literature*, Bloomington : Indiana
University Press, 1955-1958, p. 106.
Trimarchi, M., INTERNATIONAL SOCIETY OF NEUROPSYCHOPHYSIOLOGY, Via
Serpieri 11 Roma
Van Buren, E., *The Secret Of The Illuminati*
Warburtun, *Divine Legation*, vol.i. page 231. 4th edition.
Watkins, Calvert (1995). *How to Kill a Dragon: Aspects of Indo-
European Poetics*. London: Oxford University Press.
Weir Smyth, *Aeschylus, with an English translation by Herbert Weir
Smyth,* Loeb Classical Library
Wellhausen, J., *Prolegomena to the History of Ancient Israel*, Forgotten
Books, 2008
Westcott, W.W., *Numbers: Their Occult Power and Mystic Virtues*, p.37
Willis R.G., (1993). *World mythology*. Macmillan. p. 43.
Werner, Craig (2007). *Higher Ground,* Crown Publishers.
Whitehead, Alfred North, (1979). *Process and Reality*, Free Press, p. 39
Wittgenstein, Ludwig (2001) [1953]. *Philosophical Investigations* § 43.
Blackwell Publishing.
ibid. *Philosophical Investigations* § 309. Blackwell Publishing.
Witzel, M., *Vedas and Upaniṣads*, in: Flood, Gavin, ed. (2003), *The
Blackwell Companion to Hinduism*, Malden, MA
Yarker, J., *The Arcane Schools*, William Tait, London 1909.